THE ODYSSEY

The Odyssey

The Odyssey

A Play

Based on Robert Fitzgerald's translation
of *The Odyssey* by Homer

MARY ZIMMERMAN

NORTHWESTERN UNIVERSITY PRESS
EVANSTON, ILLINOIS

Northwestern University Press
www.nupress.northwestern.edu

Copyright © 2006 by Mary Zimmerman.
Published 2006 by Northwestern University Press. All rights reserved.

Printed in the United States of America

10 9 8 7 6 5 4

ISBN-13: 978-0-8101-2093-8
ISBN-10: 0-8101-2093-3

Based on *The Odyssey* by Homer, trans-
lated by Robert Fitzgerald (New York: Far-
rar, Straus and Giroux, 1998)

LIBRARY OF CONGRESS
CATALOGING-IN-PUBLICATION DATA

Zimmerman, Mary.
  The Odyssey : a play / Mary Zimmerman.
  p. cm.
  "Based on Homer's The Odyssey, trans-
lated by Robert Fitzgerald."
  ISBN 0-8101-2093-3 (pbk. : alk. paper)
  1. Odysseus (Greek mythology) Dra-
ma. I. Fitzgerald, Robert, 1910– II. Homer.
Odyssey. III. Title.
PS3576.I66O39 2005
812'.54—dc22

                    2004025480

⊗ The paper used in this publication meets
the minimum requirements of the Ameri-
can National Standard for Information Sci-
ences—Permanence of Paper for Printed
Library Materials, ANSIZ39.48-1992.

For Bruce Norris

CONTENTS

PRODUCTION HISTORY

An initial two-evening version of *The Odyssey* was produced by the Department of Performance Studies at Northwestern University in 1989. A subsequent two-evening version was produced by the Lookingglass Theatre Company in 1990 at Chicago Filmmakers. The Lookingglass cast was as follows:

Athena . . . . Eva Barr
Odysseus . . . . David Catlin
Eumaeus and others . . . . Thomas Cox
Hermes and others . . . . Larry DiStasi
Zeus and Laertes . . . . Chris Donahue
Eurycleia, Arete, Circe, and others . . . . Christine Dunford
Helen, Nausicaa, Singer, and others . . . . Laura Eason
Penelope and others . . . . Joy Gregory
Alcinous and others . . . . David Kersnar
Menelaus, Cyclops, and others . . . . David Schwimmer
Antinous, Poseidon, and others . . . . Philip R. Smith
Calypso, Melantho, and others . . . . Heidi Stillman
Telemachus and others . . . . Andy White
Musicians . . . . Eric Huffman, Temple Williams, Bruce Norris

The original music was by Eric Huffman; the film by Jenni Sioux Hopkins; the lighting design by Mark Hager. The stage manager was Whitney Blakemore. The set and costumes were by Mary Zimmerman and the company.

The world premiere of this one-evening version of *The Odyssey* opened at the Goodman Theatre, Chicago, on September 18, 1999.

Helen, Melantho, and others . . . . Anjali Bhimani

Phemios, Arete, Eurylochus, and others. . . . Antoinette Broderick

Laertes . . . . Nathan Davis

Zeus, Cyclops, and Demodocus . . . . Ed Dixon

Odysseus . . . . Christopher Donahue

Hermes and others . . . . Kyle Hall

Telemachus and others . . . . Doug Hara

Penelope and others . . . . Felicity Jones

Eteoneus, Leodes, and others . . . . Chris Kipiniak

Denizen of Heaven, Circe, and others . . . . Louise Lamson

Athena . . . . Mariann Mayberry

Neoman, Ladonis, and others . . . . Andrew Navarro

Antinous and others . . . . David New

Poseidon and others . . . . Jonathan Partington

Menelaus, Mentor, and others . . . . Yasen Peyankov

Nausicaa and others . . . . Geryll Robinson

Muse, Calypso, Argos, Aiolos, and others . . . . Heidi Stillman

Aeolus and others . . . . Paul Oakley Stovall

Eurycleia, Odysseus's Mother, and others . . . . Lisa Tejero

Eumaeus . . . . Gary Wingert

Alcinous and others . . . . Dexter Zollicoffer

Set design. . . . . Daniel Ostling

Costume design . . . . Mara Blumenfeld

Lighting design . . . . T. J. Gerckens

Sound design . . . . Michael Bodeen

Original music composition . . . . Michael Bodeen and
Willie Schwarz

Film . . . . John Boesche

Additional choreography . . . . Kristen Showalter

Production stage manager . . . . Joseph Drummond

Stage manager . . . . T. Paul Lynch

The Odyssey was subsequently produced at the McCarter Theatre, Princeton, New Jersey, and the Seattle Repertory Theatre in 2000.

All productions were directed by Mary Zimmerman.

A NOTE ON THE ADAPTATION

I chose to base my adaptation on Robert Fitzgerald's brilliant translation of Homer's *Odyssey* because it's the one I grew up with and the one I love. For me, who doesn't speak a word of Greek, Fitzgerald's *Odyssey* simply is *The Odyssey*, and, right or wrong, I feel a devotion to it similar to that which some people feel to the King James Bible. Still, I know that fellow lovers of Fitzgerald and *The Odyssey* will find things to grumble about in my adaptation.

First, I don't preserve Fitzgerald's careful phonetic spellings of and diacritical marks in proper names. Why not? Because I found in the rehearsal room that doing so befuddled the actors and made them grumpy. They kept stopping and looking at me accusingly whenever they came to any proper name—which was all the time. When I switched to a more familiar, anglicized spelling, the actors brightened and were free to shift their anxiety to something else. I believe this would be the case with any cast.

Second, even in passages that are almost verbatim from Fitzgerald, my line breaks are not always consistent with his, and this is because of tiny cuts and shifts in language and syntax, which are part of the process of adaptation.

Third, the play is long but not as long as the poem. I had to make agonizing cuts in the original story. Here, there are no Lastrygonians; there is a much abbreviated trip to the Underworld; Nestor is gone; there is no fight with the cowherd in the palace; there are no repentant suitors arriving in Hades ("all flitting, flitting all crisscross in the dark"); and—hardest of all for me—Penelope does not relate her dream ("From a water's edge / twenty fat geese have come") to the disguised Odysseus. All of these cuts were made in the interest of keeping the length of the play reasonable.

I have made some smaller changes, most for purely practical reasons. For instance, I substitute the name "Icmalius" for "Mentes" because Mentes and Mentor appear in quick succession, both played by the same person (Athena), which initially caused much confusion in the cast and audience alike.

Despite these notable alterations (and many more besides), I believe that the adaptation is, in the end, quite faithful to its source. I do not entirely transform the poem from the epic to the dramatic mode, preferring instead to preserve much of the narrative voice by giving it to Athena and, of course, Odysseus, in direct address to the audience; and although there are omissions, I stay true to the original structure of the tale. Although there are occasional anachronisms, and some radical solutions to the problems of staging the impossible, my intention is always to tell the story as best I can within the beautiful but strict confines of the stage.

A NOTE ON THE STAGING

The set consists of a rough, stone-colored surface ("rocky Ithaca") extending far off into the wings on either side of the proscenium opening. Two separate sets of wooden walls track on or fly in to create interiors or reshape the playing space. There is an "above" area for Penelope's chamber and another "above" for heaven, where Zeus resides throughout most of the play. Additionally, there are some white lengths of linen to be pulled onstage to serve as clouds, sails for a boat, curtains for a fancier room, or projection surfaces. All the way upstage is a white cyclorama.

Wooden chairs and bamboo poles are deployed for almost everything necessary: boats, a pen for sheep, swords, spears, oars, the axheads. Other scenic elements should be simple and emblematic; for instance, a green tree branch to indicate "we are outside" for the assembly scene, a large flower for the Lotus Eaters, a sun for the island of Helios, a wall of blue Plexiglas for the sea of Calypso's island, a fancy divan for Menelaus and Helen.

The scenes should shift with very minimal fuss. No blackouts are needed; scenes should "cross-fade" across the stage. A person turns in a new direction and is in a different location immediately. The narration (carried primarily by Athena and Odysseus) should work in relation to stage images—whether those images are detailed and realistic or fragmentary, poetic, and abstract—and very rarely simply replace or obviate staging. Sound and lights are important aids to the storytelling. (For additional staging suggestions, see the appendix, page 171.)

THE ODYSSEY

CHARACTERS

ITHACA
Odysseus
Penelope, his wife
Telemachus, his son
Laertes, his father
Eurycleia, a nurse
Phemios, a blind singer
Halitherses, Mentor, Neoman,
and other Townspeople
Antinous, Leodes, Eurymachus,
and other Suitors
Maids, in the palace of
Odysseus, including Melantho
and Alcippe
Eumaeus

PHAECIA
Alcinous, the king
Arete, his queen
Nausicaa, their daughter, and
her companions
Demodocus, a blind singer, and
other Phaecians

MOUNT OLYMPUS AND
OTHER PLACES
Zeus, lord of the heavens
Athena, his daughter
Poseidon, his brother, lord of
the ocean
Calypso, a sea nymph
Hermes, a messenger
Muse
Lotus Eaters
Aeolus, king of the winds,
and his children
Cyclops
Circe, an enchantress
Sirens
Scylla, a six-headed monster
Menelaus and Helen, king and
queen of Sparta
Proteus, the Ancient of the Sea

Additional characters include the Sailors of Telemachus, Phaecia, and Odysseus (including Elpenor, Eurylochus, and Perimedes); many Animals, enchanted and otherwise; Denizens of Heaven and the Underworld (including Teiresias and Odysseus's Mother); additional Cyclopes, Drummers, Servants, and Attendants.

ACT I

OPENING

[*A* WOMAN *comes out carrying a chair and a copy of Homer's* Odyssey. *She places the chair center stage, sits, opens the book, and begins reading, uninspired.*]

WOMAN:
Sing in me, Muse, and through me tell the story
of that man skilled in all ways of contending—

[*She stops, looks at the cover of the book, then tries again.*]

Sing in me, Muse, and through me—

[*She stops, sighs, and starts again.*]

Sing in me, Muse—

[*The* MUSE *appears, rubbing her eyes and yawning, having just been awakened. She slowly wanders up to the* WOMAN *from behind, listening.*]

Sing in me, Muse, and through me tell the story
of that man skilled in all ways of contending,
the wanderer, harried for years on end,
after he plundered the stronghold
on the proud height of Troy—

[*Suddenly the* MUSE *snatches the book and throws it away. She grabs the* WOMAN *from behind and begins to whisper in her ear. The* WOMAN, *gasping and clutching at her own heart, begins to speak in a rush, the words coming out of her in spite of herself.*]

Sing in me, Muse, and through me tell the story
of that man skilled in all ways of contending,
the wanderer, harried for years on end,
after he plundered the stronghold
on the proud height of Troy.

[*She struggles to escape the* MUSE *and falls on the floor; the chair falls over. The* MUSE *still clings to her.*]

He saw the townlands
and learned the minds of many different men,
and weathered many bitter nights and days
in his deep heart at sea, while he fought only
to save his life, to bring his shipmates home.
But not by will nor valor could he save them.

[*The* MUSE *releases the* WOMAN *and wanders off sleepily.*]

Of these adventures, Muse, daughter of Zeus,
tell us in our time, lift the great song again.

HEAVEN (MOUNT OLYMPUS)

[*Music. Enter a* DENIZEN OF HEAVEN. *The* MUSE *reenters carrying* ATHENA'*s clothes and throughout the following dresses the* WOMAN *as* ATHENA, *whom she now becomes.*]

DENIZEN OF HEAVEN:
Up on Mount Olympus, where the home of the gods
stands firm and unmoving forever, they say,
not spattered with rain, nor ever piled under the snow,
but where the shining bright clouds stretch out below,
and the white light glances upon them,
there the gods are all at home.

[*Enter* ZEUS *and* POSEIDON, *separately.* POSEIDON *carries a trident and a suitcase.*]

POSEIDON:
All but Poseidon, lord of the ocean,
who has gone to visit the Ethiopians.

[*He exits. Music ends.*]

ZEUS:
I find it so lamentable that men should blame
the gods for everything they bring upon themselves.
All their afflictions come from us, we hear.
And what of their own failings?

Take that man Aigisthos, who stole Agamemnon's wife,
then killed him the day he returned from Troy.
And yet we gods had warned him, sent down Hermes,
our most observant messenger, to say,
"Don't kill the man, don't touch his wife,
or face a reckoning with Orestes."
Friendly advice—but would Aigisthos take it?
Now he is dead, as we said he would be.

ATHENA:
O Father Zeus!

ZEUS:
Athena?

ATHENA:
O Majesty, that man is in the dust as he deserved—
let all who act as he did die that way.
But listen to me now:
My own heart is broken for Odysseus,
the master mind of war, so long a castaway
upon a tiny island in the running sea.
Calypso, the goddess there, will not let Odysseus go.
She keeps coaxing him with her beguiling talk,
to turn his mind from Ithaca, while
his only desire is to see his homeland once again.
Are you not moved by this?
Had you no pleasure from Odysseus
when he fought at Troy?
What do you hold against him now?

ZEUS:
My child, what strange remarks you make.
Could I forget Odysseus?
It's only Poseidon who bears the fighter
an old grudge, since Odysseus poked out
the eye of the Cyclops, Poseidon's son.
Naturally, the god, after the blinding—
mind you, he doesn't kill the man,
only buffets him away from home.
But come now, my brother's gone to Ethiopia;
let's take up the matter of Odysseus's return.
Poseidon must relent, for being quarrelsome
will get him nowhere.

ATHENA:
                                     O Majesty,
O Father of us all, if it now please you,
send the wayfinder, Hermes, across the sea
to Calypso's island. Let him tell the nymph
with the pretty braids that she must let Odysseus go.

ZEUS:
We shall do it.

ATHENA:
                          We must act soon!
There is a wolf pack of suitors at Odysseus's door
harassing his wife, Penelope, for her hand,
destroying his house, making wantons of his maids,
and eating up his property. His son Telemachus
can do nothing against them.

ZEUS:

That's no good.

ATHENA:
I'll go to Ithaca, stir up Telemachus,
send him to the mainland, to Sparta,
for news of his father. In this way,
he may win his own renown about the world.

ZEUS:
An excellent plan. Farewell, my child.

[ZEUS *goes up to Mount Olympus, where he will remain, watching all the action below. The* MUSE *enters with* ATHENA's *golden sandals and a long spear and hands them to her. Music.*]

MUSE:
Athena bends to tie her beautiful sandals on,
ambrosial, golden, that carry her over water
or over endless land on the wings of the wind,
and takes the great haft of her spear in hand—
she goes in disguise toward Ithaca, home of
the lost Odysseus, where his son waits fatherless
and his wife, Penelope, is harassed by suitors for her hand.

VISITATION

[*New music, drumming. Ithaca: the palace of Odysseus. All the* SUITORS *enter together, moving slowly. Then, as the music grows and accelerates, they disperse and begin to tear up the place. They fling chairs around, cavort with the* MAIDS, *fight with one another.*

8

In the middle of all this, PENELOPE *and her son,* TELEMACHUS, *enter.* TELEMACHUS *wears his father's old cloak, which is too big for him.* PENELOPE *and* TELEMACHUS *hold hands, walking through the chaos of the* SUITORS *until* PENELOPE *becomes overwhelmed and runs off. Eventually the music dies away, and the* SUITORS, *exhausted, grow still. The blind singer* PHEMIOS *enters.* ATHENA, *carrying her long spear, comes into the doorway and looks around. She is disguised as* ICMALIUS, *a crusty old seadog.*]

TELEMACHUS [*spotting the new arrival*]:
Welcome, stranger. Welcome to my house. . . .
I am Telemachus.

ICMALIUS (ATHENA):
                    Young man, I've come—

TELEMACHUS:
No, please, come in and sit before you tell me
why you're here. Come this way.

[*The* SUITORS *make a loud disturbance.*]

I apologize for them; they have an easy life,
living off the livestock of another.

[*He sets up two chairs as he speaks. They sit.*]

                              But where
do you come from? Is Ithaca new to you,
or were you a guest here in the old days?

ICMALIUS (ATHENA):
My name is Icmalius. I'm the captain of a ship
I've moored on a wild strip of coast nearby,
under a wooded mountain. You don't remember,
but years back, my family and yours were friends.
As for my sailing here—the tale was that Odysseus
had come home; therefore I came.

[*The* SUITORS *make a disturbance.*]

I see the gods delay him.

TELEMACHUS:
Don't say "delay," my friend, he's lost;
his bones are rotting somewhere now,
white in the rain on dark earth where they lie,
or tumbling in the groundswell of the sea.
There's no help in hoping he'll come back.
That sun has long gone down.

ICMALIUS (ATHENA):
But never in this world is Odysseus dead—

TELEMACHUS:
Sir—

ICMALIUS (ATHENA):
—only detained somewhere on the wide sea,
upon some island, with wild islanders;
savages they must be to hold him captive.

TELEMACHUS:
Sir, rest assured you shall have my hospitality.
You needn't—

ICMALIUS (ATHENA):
                        Listen to me, young man—

TELEMACHUS:
—say what you think I want—

ICMALIUS (ATHENA):
                                    —I will forecast for you,
for the gods have put a strong feeling in me.

TELEMACHUS:
You are my guest: go on, if it gives you pleasure.

ICMALIUS (ATHENA):
I see it all: Odysseus will not, now,
be long away from Ithaca. Even if he is in chains
he'll scheme a way to come. He can do anything.

TELEMACHUS:
You are very kind, sir.

ICMALIUS (ATHENA):
Ah yes, I can see you are Odysseus's boy—
the way your head is shaped, your fine eyes,
and your suspicions.

TELEMACHUS:

Yes, they say I am
Odysseus's son; but I say I wish I had instead
some simple happy man for a father,
growing old here in his own home.

[*The* SUITORS *make a disturbance.*]

ICMALIUS (ATHENA) [*rising*]:
Who are these men? They seem so arrogant!
Making pigs of themselves in your father's house.
A sensible man would blush to be among them.

TELEMACHUS:
They are lords of all the other islands
here courting my mother; they use our house
as if it were a house to plunder. My mother hates them all,
but we don't dare turn them away—we are too far
outnumbered.

Here is my forecast:
They will destroy everything we have,
and as soon as they can, they will kill me
and one of them will take my mother.

ICMALIUS (ATHENA):
Perhaps it is well Odysseus is delayed.
His heart would break to hear you speak like this.

TELEMACHUS:
He's gone, my friend, the whirlwinds have him.

ICMALIUS (ATHENA):
If I were you, I'd take steps to make these men disperse.

TELEMACHUS:
Take steps? I haven't—

ICMALIUS (ATHENA):
At daybreak call the islanders to assembly:
the suitors must go scattering to their homes.
Then here's the course for you, if you agree:
get a sound ship afloat with twenty oars
and go abroad for news of your lost father.
Go ask King Menelaus and his wife Helen of Troy—
they are both now back at home.

TELEMACHUS:
                              But I don't—

ICMALIUS (ATHENA):
If you should learn your father is alive
and coming home, you could hold out another year.
But if you learn that he is dead and gone,
come home and raise a mound for him,
burn his gear, and give your mother to another man.
Then decide how to avenge yourself on all of these—
how you should kill them—outright or with guile.

TELEMACHUS:
I don't know, I—

[*Suddenly* ATHENA *is young and vital. She grabs* TELEMACHUS *forcefully.*]

ICMALIUS (ATHENA) [*whispering*]:
                    Listen to me, Telemachus:
You cannot go on clinging to your childhood.
You are not of an age to do that.

[*She releases him and reassumes her elderly manner.*]

                    Dear friend,
I can see that you are splendid. Be brave as well,
and men in times to come will speak of you respectfully.

TELEMACHUS:
I thank you for your counsel, Icmalius. I do thank you.

ICMALIUS (ATHENA):
I must rejoin my ship; my crew grumbles
when I keep them waiting.

TELEMACHUS:
You must get back to sea, I know, but come
and have a hot bath and rest; accept a gift—

ICMALIUS (ATHENA):
Please do not delay me, for I love the sea ways.

[*She turns and suddenly flies off. The* SUITORS *do not see, but* TELEMACHUS *does.*]

TELEMACHUS [*to himself*]:
A god has been my guest.

[*Music.* PHEMIOS *begins to sing.* PENELOPE *enters above and overhears.*]

PHEMIOS:
Odysseus sailed on the wine-dark sea
to the shadowed heights of Troy,
bravest of men, most skilled of men,
but now he'll come no more—

PENELOPE [*interrupting*]:
Phemios, I know you know some other songs
of gods and heroes. Sing no more
this bitter tale that wears my heart away.
It opens in me again the wound of longing
for one incomparable, ever in my mind—

TELEMACHUS:
Mother, why do you begrudge our own dear Phemios
the joy of song, wherever his thought may lead?
Poets are not to blame, but Zeus, who gives
what fate he pleases to adventurous men.
You must be brave, Mother, and try to listen.

PENELOPE:
Who is this speaking? Is this my son?
I would have thought Odysseus had returned—
your voice the very echo of his own. Dear Phemios,
Telemachus is right: sing what you will
and I must learn to bear it.

[PENELOPE *exits.*]

TELEMACHUS [*approaching the* SUITORS]:
You suitors of my mother!
It's time for you to go on home!
At daybreak we shall sit down in assembly
and I shall tell you—take it as you will—
you are to leave this hall. Go feasting elsewhere,
consume your own stores! Turn and turn about,
use one another's houses! If you choose
to slaughter one man's livestock and pay nothing,
by the eternal gods you shall get what you deserve!

ANTINOUS:
Telemachus, no doubt the gods themselves
are teaching you this high and mighty manner.
Zeus forbid you should be king in Ithaca—

TELEMACHUS:
Antinous, you may not like my answer,
but I would happily be king. A king
will be respected, and his house will flourish.
But if my father's dead, and the gods decree
that someone else should come to power,
then I still insist that I rule my own house.

ANTINOUS:
Telemachus, who knows who will be king in Ithaca?
But keep your property, and rule your house,
and let no man, against your will, make havoc
with your possessions.
                    But now, my brave
young friend, a question or two about that stranger.
Where did your guest come from? Of what country?

SUITOR ONE:
Had he some message of your father's coming,
or business of his own?

SUITOR TWO:
                              He left so quickly that one
hadn't time to meet him, but he seemed a gentleman.

TELEMACHUS:
You all know there is no hope for my father;
I wouldn't trust a message, if one came,
nor any prophet my mother invites
to tell our fortune. My guest was Icmalius—
a family friend.

ATHENA [*entering*]:
So said Telemachus, though in his heart
he knew his guest had been immortal.
He was lying and, like his father, he did it well.
But now the suitors turned to play again.
They stayed till nightfall,
then half asleep they left, each for his home.

NIGHTTIME

[SUITORS *exit.* EURYCLEIA, *an old servant, enters with* TELEMACHUS'*s
nightclothes. Throughout the following, he undresses and prepares
for bed, aided by* EURYCLEIA.]

TELEMACHUS:

Eurycleia, before me you nursed my father,
and I think you know him best of all. Tell me,
do you think he could still come home?

EURYCLEIA:

I don't tell fortunes, dear Telemachus.
It will happen or it won't, as the gods decide.
But you can be certain, whether he is in this world
or the next, that his heart longs for you. Remember
when they came to take him to the fields of Troy
he pretended he was mad—

TELEMACHUS:

       I know, I know.

EURYCLEIA:

He pretended he was mad by going to our fields
and sowing them with salt. But then they found you,
little baby that you were, and placed you
right in the path of his plow—

TELEMACHUS:

And he turned the plow aside.

EURYCLEIA:

        Yes.
He turned the plow aside for your sake,
Telemachus. And then they knew
he was not mad, and off he had to go.

TELEMACHUS:
Good night, my sweet.

EURYCLEIA:
Good night.

ASSEMBLY AND DEPARTURE

[*Music. It is morning.* TELEMACHUS *rises.* ATHENA *enters. As she speaks, the* SUITORS, *two* MAIDS, *and* TOWNSPEOPLE, *including* MEN- TOR, *who wears an eyepatch, and* HALITHERSES, *enter with chairs for the assembly. They sit.* TELEMACHUS *stands on a chair before them.*]

ATHENA:
When primal dawn spread on the eastern sky
her fingers of pink light, Odysseus's true son
stood up, drew on his tunic, and left his room,
a god's brilliance upon him. The criers' call sang out,
and the men came streaming onto the assembly ground.
He entered and Athena lavished on him a sunlit grace.

TOWNSPERSON:
Telemachus, tell us why you have called this meeting.
Do you have news of our army? Will it return from Troy?

TELEMACHUS:
I have no news of our troops returning
nor any public business to propose;
only my need, and the trouble of my house.
My home and all I have are being ruined.
Mother wanted no suitors, but like a pack

they came—men with no stomach for an introduction
to Icarios, her father across the sea.
Where is our power to expel them all alone?
My house is being plundered, and you stand by.
Think of the talk in the islands all around us.
Where is your shame? Or did my father, Odysseus,
ever do you injury? How can these dogs—

[ANTINOUS *applauds, slowly, and rises.*]

ANTINOUS:
What rhetoric, Telemachus! No holding you.
You want to shame us, and humiliate us,
yet you know the suitors are not to blame—
but your own dear mother, the incomparable queen
of cunning. For three years now—and it will soon be four—
she has been breaking the hearts of the Acheans,
holding out hope to all, answering to none.
Wits like Penelope's never were before—
history cannot show the like among the ringleted
ladies of Achea. Her lying tricks and strategems
have kept us off till now. She makes a name for herself,
but you can feel the loss it means for you.
Now here's the suitors' answer—burn it in your mind:
Dismiss your mother from the house, or make her
marry the man her father names.

TELEMACHUS:
                                    Antinous,
I will not cast my mother out.
Find your dinner elsewhere.

ATHENA:
Now Zeus who views the wide world sent a sign,

[*Music.* ZEUS *stands above, removes two feathers from a box, and tosses them down from heaven.*]

launching a pair of eagles from a mountain.
They wheeled above the assembly,
tearing at each other, and their feathers floated down.

HALITHERSES [*coming forward*]:
Hear me, Ithacans! I am old enough
to know a sign when I see one, and I say
that all has come to pass for Odysseus
as I foretold when he set sail. He will come home—
he is even now at hand—

ANTINOUS:
                        Enough, old man!
Go home and read omens to your children!
There's bird life aplenty in the sunny air, not all
of it significant. Here, let me interpret.

[*He takes the feathers.*]

Odysseus is dead, and I wish you were with him—
then we'd be spared this "divination."
Telemachus, send your mother to her father's house
to marry the man he names!

TELEMACHUS:

                    I'm done, Antinous.
I am done.

ANTINOUS:

          Well, thank the gods for that.
We'll see you soon at home.

[*All exit except* TELEMACHUS *and one of the people of the town,*
MENTOR.]

TELEMACHUS:
Good Lord Mentor, a word with you.
I mean to make a trip to Sparta, to find out news
of my father. Can you help me? Find me a ship—
to sail tonight in secret?

MENTOR:

                    Telemachus, your father and I—

TELEMACHUS:
Were best of friends, I know. Can you do it?

MENTOR:
I believe Neoman has a ship in port.
I'll do my best.

TELEMACHUS:

               Thank you, friend.
Then I'm going home to make provisions.
Meet me at midnight at the docks.

[MENTOR *exits.* TELEMACHUS *turns, and now he is at home.* EURYCLEIA *enters.*]

Nurse, get a few two-handled traveling jugs
filled up with wine—the second best.
And pour out barley into leather bags—
twenty bushels' worth. Now keep this to yourself!
I'm off to Sparta to see what news there is of Father.

EURYCLEIA:
Dear child, whatever put this in your head?
Why do you want to go so far in the world—
and you our only darling? Think how, when you
have turned your back, these men will plot to kill you!

TELEMACHUS:
Take heart, Nurse, there's a god behind this plan.
And you must swear to keep it from my mother
until the eleventh day, or twelfth, or till
she misses me, or hears I'm gone.
She must not tear her lovely skin lamenting.

[*Music.* EURYCLEIA *exits.* ATHENA *enters.*]

ATHENA:
The sun was sinking and darkness fell.
The gray-eyed one roamed the town
disguised as Telemachus, gathering sailors
and begging a ship of Neoman. She found
the good Lord Mentor, cast him into
forgetfulness, and took his form to meet Telemachus.

[ATHENA *is now* MENTOR *and wears an eyepatch. She meets up with* TELEMACHUS *as* SAILORS *enter with chairs to make a ship.*]

Come, Captain, your ship is waiting.

[SAILORS, ATHENA, *and* TELEMACHUS *board* NEOMAN's *ship. The music quickens. They set off. The* SAILORS *row briskly.*]

ATHENA:
The sun rose on the flawless brimming sea
into a sky all golden—and facing sunrise
the voyagers now lay off Lakedaimon. Here
they put in, furled sail, and beached the ship:
already they could see in the distance the
incomparable palace of Menelaus and his lady Helen.

[*The* SAILORS *disperse. Music ends.* ATHENA *and* TELEMACHUS *approach the palace of* MENELAUS.]

MENELAUS

TELEMACHUS:
Mentor, how can I do it? How approach him?
For a young man to interrogate an older man
seems so disrespect—

MENTOR (ATHENA):
              Telemachus,
no shyness now. You came across
the open sea for this.

TELEMACHUS:
What should I say?

MENTOR (ATHENA):
Reason and heart will give you some words, and
the gods will give you others, I guarantee.
They are not indifferent to your life.

[ETEONUS *enters and sees the visitors. He returns to* MENELAUS, *who
has entered with* HELEN.]

ETEONUS:
Lord Menelaus, Lady Helen, two men are here—
two strangers, though they appear nobly born.
Shall we bring them in or send them on?

MENELAUS:
You were no idiot before, Eteonus.
What happened? Could we have made it home
from Troy if other men had never fed us,
given us lodging? Bring them in.

ETEONUS:
Strangers, you are welcome. Please, follow me.

TELEMACHUS:
My friend, can you believe your eyes?
All the bronze, gold infused with silver, ivory!
This is the way the court of Zeus must look.

[ATHENA *exchanges a wry glance with* ZEUS, *observing from above.*]

MENELAUS [*overhearing and approaching*]:
Young friend, no mortal man can vie with Zeus.
His home and all his treasures are forever.
As for men, it's true that few have more than I.

TELEMACHUS:
My lord marshall Menelaus, how fortunate you are.

MENELAUS:
Fortunate? While I was off in Troy, in Cyprus,
and in Egypt gathering all of this, a stranger killed
my brother in cold blood, and many of my companions
perished on the sea. What pleasure can I take, then,
being lord over all these costly things?

HELEN:
My lord, shall I say what I think?

MENELAUS:
Please, my lady Helen.

HELEN:
Never, anywhere, have I seen so great a likeness
—but it is truly strange!
This boy must be the son of Odysseus,
Telemachus, the child he left at home
the year the Achean host made war on Troy—
daring all for the wanton that I was.

MENTOR (ATHENA):
This is that hero's son as you surmise,
and I am his old friend, Lord Mentor.

MENELAUS:
Odysseus's son in my house?

HELEN:
I would know him anywhere. Do you remember,
Lord, how Odysseus once beat himself, dressed
in rags, and slipped into the Trojan city to
spy among his enemies? So changed he looked,
and no one there remarked him. But I knew him—
even as he was, I knew him—and questioned him.
How shrewdly he put me off.

MENELAUS:
In my life I have met, in many countries,
many brilliant men, but never one like Odysseus.

TELEMACHUS:
Lord Marshall Menelaus, I came to hear
what news you have of Father.
Tell me of his death, sir, if perhaps
you witnessed it. Spare me no part
for kindness' sake.

MENELAUS:
I'll tell you everything I know.

[*Distant music. The figures of* YOUNG MENELAUS, EIDOTHEA, *and* PROTEUS *appear upstage, carrying small pyramids which they set down. As* MENELAUS *recalls each of them they enact his story on the past, upstage.*]

It happened in Egypt, on the island called Pharos.
Here the gods held me twenty days becalmed.
No winds came up. Stranded, my men and I
were failing. But then a goddess intervened—
Eidothea, daughter of Proteus, the Ancient of the Sea.

EIDOTHEA:
Sir,

MENELAUS:
she said to me,

EIDOTHEA:
are you a fool? Are you weak in the head?
Or is it because you like to suffer that you allow
yourself to be cooped up all this time on the island?

MENELAUS:
To this I quickly answered:

YOUNG MENELAUS:
                              Let me assure you,
Goddess, whatever goddess you may be,
I have no wish to linger here.
How am I to make my voyage home?

EIDOTHEA:
The island is haunted by the Ancient of the Sea.

[PROTEUS, *the Ancient of the Sea, enters.*]

At noon each day he glides ashore and lies
sleeping like a shepherd with his flock of seals.
If you can take him by surprise and hold him fast,
he'll give you course and distance for your sailing
homeward across the cold fish-breeding sea.

MENELAUS:
I followed her instructions—I still recall
the stench of those damned seals. I sprang
upon him, but his tricks were not knocked out of him.
First, he took on a lion's shape, then a serpent's,
a leopard's, a great boar's, then fire and water.
But I held on, and finally, exhausted, he resumed
his shape. I asked him why I was high and dry so long
upon the island.

PROTEUS:
                You blundered. You should
have paid honor to Zeus and the other gods,
a proper sacrifice, before embarking. You must
travel the Nile once again and make the offerings.

MENELAUS:
But then I asked him, as the gods know all:

YOUNG MENELAUS:
What of my companions? Have they had a safe return?
What of Agamemnon, my brother, and Odysseus, my friend?

MENELAUS:
And he answered that my brother had been killed
when he came home. My heart was broken down.

I slumped on the trampled sand and cried aloud.
But even then I wished to hear:

YOUNG MENELAUS:
What of Odysseus?

MENELAUS:
And the Ancient said,

PROTEUS:
I saw him weeping, weeping on an island.
He has no means of sailing home,
but stares out at the barren sea,
watching his sweet life drain away.

[*The scene of Egypt fades away.*]

ATHENA:
Now all the company grew sad to hear this tale;
then it entered Helen's mind
to drop into the wine an anodyne, mild magic
of forgetfulness. Whoever drank would be incapable
of tears or sorrow all that night—though he should lose
both mother and father or his child.
They drifted off, pulled by the swelling tide of sleep,
deep into the mansion; and there lay down
under purple rugs and the glistening stars.

[*Music ends.*]

NEOMAN

[*Drums. The scene shifts back to Ithaca, outside the palace.* ANTI-
NOUS *and two other* SUITORS *are practicing throwing a javelin when
they are interrupted by* NEOMAN, *a townsperson.*]

NEOMAN:
Do any of you know what day Telemachus
is coming home from Sparta?
He took my ship and I need it back
to make a cruise to Elis. I have a dozen mares
at pasture there. My notion is to bring one home—

[*The* SUITORS *converge threateningly on* NEOMAN.]

ANTINOUS:
I want the truth! He sailed? To Sparta? Who joined him—
a crew he picked up here in Ithaca
or his own servants? Did he force your ship
from you or did you give it?

NEOMAN:
I gave it to him freely! Who wouldn't,
when a prince of that house asks for it?
His crew was of the best men on the island—
aside from yourselves. I saw Mentor go aboard—
or, I don't know, it might have been some god
that looked like him. The strange thing is
I saw Lord Mentor here yesterday at dawn,
although they sailed five days ago for Sparta—

ANTINOUS [*backing off*]:
So he had the guts to make the crossing;
he finds a crew, in spite of us, and puts to sea?
What will he do next?

[NEOMAN *runs off.*]

Just get me a fast ship and twenty men;
we'll intercept him in the strait:
he'll find his father—underneath the sea.

[*The* SUITORS *exit.*]

PENELOPE'S DREAM

[*Drums. Music.* PENELOPE's *bedroom.* EURYCLEIA *is with* PENELOPE.]

PENELOPE:
Why has my child left me? He had no need
to go off on the broad back of the sea.
What was he thinking? Why did he go?
Must he too be lost and forgotten?

EURYCLEIA:
Perhaps a god moved him—who knows?—
or his own heart sent him to Sparta.

PENELOPE:
If I had seen that sailing in his eyes
he should have stayed with me, for all his longing.

Stayed—or left me dead in the great hall.
You knew the hour he took the black ship out to sea!
Why didn't you wake me?

EURYCLEIA [*dramatically, struggling to kneel*]:
Sweet mistress, have my throat cut without mercy—

PENELOPE:
Would that bring him back?

EURYCLEIA [*getting up*]:
                              He made me swear
a great oath to tell you nothing till twelve days
went by, or till you heard of it yourself. He was afraid
you'd tear your skin in lamentation. Come, come.
It's in the hands of the gods, and Telemachus believes
he has one by his side. Lie down now,
go to sleep. Here, lie down, now. Sleep.

[PENELOPE *lies down.* EURYCLEIA *begins to leave, but* PENELOPE
reaches for her, and EURYCLEIA *lies down near her. Music.* PENELOPE
dreams of her SISTER, *who is* ATHENA *in disguise.*]

SISTER (ATHENA):
Are you sleeping, sorrowing Penelope?
The gods cannot bear to see you cry.
Your son will soon return. He's done no wrong.

PENELOPE:
Sister, what brings you here? You live so far away
I never see you anymore. Do you know
what has happened? I saw my lord, my lion,

carried on a ship, and I have never seen him since.
And now my son has sailed away and left me all alone.

SISTER (ATHENA):
Lift up your heart, don't be afraid.
Pallas Athena is with your son, and loves him.
It is she who sent me here to tell you this.

PENELOPE:
If you are truly heaven-sent, and hear
the voices of gods, then tell me, tell me, please:
Is my husband alive or dead?
Is he ever coming home?

SISTER (ATHENA) [*departing*]:
Of Odysseus, I may not speak.

CALYPSO

[*Music. Calypso's island. Blue sky.* CALYPSO *is playing solitaire. On her wrist is tied one end of a long rope which trails off to something out of sight.* HERMES *enters on a bike, ringing the handlebar bell. He is dressed like a bike messenger, with winged feet. Music ends.*]

CALYPSO:
Hermes! What brings you here? You hardly
ever come! Come inside and say what's on
your mind, and if I can I'll help you.

[*She sits him down and fetches tea as he speaks.*]

HERMES:

I was sent. You think I'd come otherwise?
Who would come over all that water
if someone didn't make him? It was unending.
Not a single city on the way, no mortals
to make sacrifices, nothing to do.
But when Zeus makes up his mind—

[*He glances up at* ZEUS.]

CALYPSO:

Zeus? What does he want with me?

HERMES:

He says you have some man here left over from Troy.
Ten years ago he did something to offend Poseidon
and there's been trouble ever since. Now it seems
Athena wants him home, and Zeus agrees.
You have to let him go and give him transport.

CALYPSO:

What monsters you are!

HERMES:

                        Excuse me?

CALYPSO:

You gods who live up in the sky! You can't bear
to see a goddess sleeping with a man, even if she lives
in the middle of the ocean and has no one else for company!
You're pretty slack yourselves with earthy girls,
but when it comes to us—!

HERMES [*glancing up at* ZEUS]:
>   Calypso—

CALYPSO:
So radiant Dawn once took to bed Orion
until you easeful gods grew peevish at it,
and holy Artemis, Artemis throned in gold,
hunted him down in Delos with her arrows.
Then Demeter yielded to Iasion, but Zeus found out
and killed him with a thunderbolt!
So now you grudge me, too, my mortal friend.
But it was I who saved him—when all his troops were lost,
his good companions—the wind and current washed him
here to me. I fed him, loved him, sang that he should
not die nor grow old, ever, in all the days to come.
But now there's no eluding Zeus's will if he insists.

HERMES:
He does insist.

CALYPSO:
>   But surely I cannot
"send" him. I have no long-oared ships, no company
to pull him on the broad back of the sea. I live alone.

HERMES:
He is to build his own ship, and you're to help.

CALYPSO:
All right, I'll let him go. I'll help him build his ship.
Go on, get out of here. You've given me your message. Go on!

HERMES:
Send him off at once, Calypso. And show more grace
in your obedience, or one day we might get annoyed
and punish you.

[*He starts to ride off.*]

CALYPSO:

Farewell, winged giant-slayer!

[ODYSSEUS *is revealed at the other end of* CALYPSO*'s rope. He is sitting
with the rope around his neck, his back to us, staring at the sea.*]

CALYPSO:
Unhappy friend, come here.

ODYSSEUS:
Calypso, please.

CALYPSO:
It's not for that, Odysseus. I don't want
anything from you. Odysseus, your unhappiness
has just ended. You're going home.

ODYSSEUS:
Don't tease me, sweet Calypso.

CALYPSO:
You're going home. No need to grieve, no need
to feel your life consumed here. I have pondered it,
and I shall help you go.
Come and cut down high timber for a raft

so you can ride her on the misty sea.
Come, I'll help you—

ODYSSEUS:

                        After all these years,
a helping hand? O Goddess, what guile is hidden here?
A raft, you say, to cross the Western Ocean,
rough water and unknown? Seaworthy ships
that glory in god's wind will never cross it.
I take no raft you grudge me out to sea.
Or yield me first a great oath, if I do,
to work no more enchantment to my harm.

CALYPSO:
What a dog you are to think of such a thing!
My witness then be earth and sky
and dripping Styx that I swear by,
I have no further spells to work against you.
Come, Odysseus, my heart is not a piece of stone.

[CALYPSO *removes the rope from* ODYSSEUS's *neck. He begins to build his boat from bamboo poles. Silently,* CALYPSO *tags along. She interferes with his work: drapes her body over his, lies on his supplies. She is always underfoot. He remains intent on his task, removing her physically from himself, from the boat as it is constructed. There is no sound but that of the ocean and gulls. In the end, he takes a ribbon from her hair to complete the binding of the boat and the tablecloth from her tea table for a sail and sets off.*]

For seventeen nights and days Odysseus
sailed on the open sea without incident.
But on the eighteenth, the dark shoreline

of Phaecia appeared. Poseidon, storming home
over the mountains of Asia with his thunderclouds,
saw him, grew sullen, and said,

[POSEIDON *enters with his suitcase, his triton, and two* DRUMMERS.]

POSEIDON:
Here's a pretty cruise! So I only had to
go to Ethiopia for the gods to change their
minds about that man. Still, I can give him
a rough ride in, and will.

CALYPSO:
                        The sky began to darken,
and it began to rain.

[CALYPSO *exits. The* DRUMMERS *drum.* POSEIDON *attacks* ODYSSEUS,
tears his boat apart, and tosses him around. Just as all seems lost,
ATHENA *enters, pulls* ODYSSEUS *away, and fends off* POSEIDON. *The
drumming slows and diminishes.*]

POSEIDON:
                        Always in trouble,
all over the seas, wherever you go, Odysseus!

[*He exits. The* DRUMMERS *remain.*]

ATHENA:
Sleep well, Odysseus. You are safe ashore,
in the land of the Phaecians.

[*They exit as* ALCINOUS *enters.* NAUSICAA *and her* COMPANIONS *enter carrying pillows and lie down to sleep.*]

PHAECIA: NAUSICAA

ALCINOUS:
So the long-suffering great Odysseus sleeps exhausted
in this place while Athena makes her way to the city
of the Phaecians. In days gone by, these men lived
in Hyperia, next to the Cyclopes. But Cyclopes
are too overbearing, being greater in strength than most,
and the Phaecians were forced to migrate here to Scheria,
where they are now ruled by King Alcinous.
It is to this king's house Athena goes.

ATHENA [*flying in*]:
Full of plans to get Odysseus home.

ALCINOUS:
She finds a painted bedchamber where a young girl
lies fast asleep. This is the daughter of Alcinous,
the princess Nausicaa. On either side, looking like the Graces,
her companions are sleeping with her.

ATHENA [*appearing to* NAUSICAA *as her closest friend*]:
Wake up! Wake up! Nausicaa, look at your clothes
and linen! How can you let everything get so dirty
and still call yourself your mother's daughter?
Leaving your clothes uncared for, Nausicaa,
when you need a whole store of marriage linen—

and soon you'll need a wedding dress! And here
you are with dirty clothes! Let's go washing
by the river. Go ask your father if you can! Go on!

[NAUSICAA *runs to her* FATHER, *and her* COMPANIONS *stir and rise.*]

NAUSICAA:
Dear Papa, I must take all our things and get them
washed at the river pools. Our linen is all soiled!
And you should wear fresh clothing, going to council
with counselors and the first men of the realm.
Everything is lying about all dirty! Remember
your five sons at home: though two are married,
we still have three bachelors, and they must
have laundered clothes each time they go dancing!
See what I must think of! I must go down to the water!

ALCINOUS:
Enough, enough, my child. I'm servant to your desires.
Go along now, the grooms will bring your wagon
with the pretty wheels. Go on. Be careful—

NAUSICAA:
I will!

[*She runs off with her* COMPANIONS, *who pull a little red wagon holding the laundry.*]

ALCINOUS:
Down by our lower shores, where Nausicaa is going,
there are running pools of water that no dirt can withstand.

And when the young girls go down there, do you know
how they wash their clothes? They dance on them!

[*The* DRUMMERS *now play to accompany* NAUSICAA *and her* COM-
PANIONS. *The* COMPANIONS *dance about with one another and on
the laundry as they chant. They toss around a red ball, playing
keep-away from* NAUSICAA. ATHENA *mingles with them, invisible to
all but the audience.*]

COMPANIONS:
Down by the seashore
the sunny seaside
we come a-washing
a-washing for the future bride

She is the highest
She will delight us
She's got the best charms
She's got the brightest arms

Come on, come on to me, girl!
You know, you got them whirling—

Come on, come on, hey!
Soon there'll be a wedding day,

Let's go, she told me, told me
Let's go, now hold me, hold me

Soon there'll be a wedding day,
Soon there'll be a wedding day.

Here he comes
Here he comes
O Nausicaa, O Nausicaa!

ODYSSEUS [*awakening*]:
Alas! What country have I come to now?
And what is this shrill echo in my ears
as if some girls were shrieking?

[ATHENA *intercepts the ball and drops it near* ODYSSEUS. NAUSICAA
follows and sees the half-naked, half-drowned man.]

ALCINOUS:
The two of them both thought,

NAUSICAA AND ODYSSEUS:
Human or divine?

ALCINOUS:
Odysseus seemed somewhat

NAUSICAA:
                       like a god.

ALCINOUS:
But also like

NAUSICAA:
             a drowned cat.

ODYSSEUS:

Mistress, please, are you a goddess or a girl?
If you're a goddess, you must be Artemis—
you have such grace in playing. But if you are a girl,
how blessed your father and your gentle mother,
how lucky your brothers. How their eyes
must brim with tears each time they see
their wondrous child go dancing!
I've been on the sea for nineteen days, and yet—

NAUSICAA:

Hush, stranger! It's clear to me you have no evil in you.
You've come to the land of the Phaecians,
and I myself am Nausicaa, daughter of our king Alcinous.
While you're here, of course ,we'll give you everything.

[*The* COMPANIONS, *feeling shy, are sneaking off.*]

Stop my maids! Why are you running away?
How can you take this poor man for an enemy?
No, he's just a poor castaway, and we must take care of him:
"Treat our strangers as we treat ourselves."
Up with you now, friend, back to town we go,
and I shall send you in before my father
who is wondrous wise. But listen: here's how we must do it.
While we go through the countryside stay with us.
But near the town, where the boatyards are, fall back,
because there are plenty of vulgar men there and I can
imagine one of them saying:

NAUSICAA AND ONE OF THE DRUMMERS:

Who is this tall and handsome stranger Nausicaa

has in tow? Where did she pick him up?
Her future husband, no doubt. Are we not good enough for her?

NAUSICAA:
This is the way they might make light of me.

[*She is suddenly embarrassed.*]

Come on. Now, remember, fall back and give us time
to reach the palace, but don't worry, you can find it on your own.
Any small child could show you the way.
And when you meet my mother and father, don't be afraid.
Remember, "a cheerful man does best in any enterprise!"

[*They all head off.*]

ALCINOUS:
And so Odysseus goes with the laundry and the wagon
and the girls toward the Phaecian city.

[*Music.*]

PHAECIA: THE CITY AND THE GAMES

[*All the* PHAECIANS *including* NAUSICAA *and her* COMPANIONS *enter and sit in their great hall. They are playful, laughing and carrying on.* ALCINOUS *and his queen,* ARETE, *sit in chairs.* ODYSSEUS *appears and, shoved forward by the invisible* ATHENA, *throws himself before them. The music and activity stop abruptly.*]

ODYSSEUS:
Great Queen, here is a man bruised by adversity,
thrown upon your mercy and the king your husband's,
begging indulgence of this company.
Grant me passage to my fatherland.

ALCINOUS [*gently*]:
Come, my good friend.

[*He helps* ODYSSEUS *to his own chair, then addresses the* PHAECIANS.]

My friends, my lords and ladies of Phaecia,
hear now all that my heart would have me say.
Our guest and new friend—nameless to me still—
comes to my house after long wandering.
He appeals to us for conveyance home.
As is our custom, therefore, let us provide passage,
and quickly, no matter how far his land may be.
What do you say? Who agrees?

[*Everyone votes yes.*]

My friends, how lucky we are, the gods have blessed us
with a guest, to entertain and to serve—
or who knows? Perhaps he is a god himself.

ODYSSEUS:
Alcinous, you may set your mind at rest. A most
unlikely god am I, being all of earth and mortal nature.
I could tell you a long tale of sorrow, but all I wish
is to be fed, to rest, and then to be taken home.

ALCINOUS:
You are right—

ARETE:
But may I ask you, stranger, just one question?

ODYSSEUS:
Yes, anything.

ARETE:
Where, friend, did you get those clothes?

ODYSSEUS:
I have been on the sea for twenty-two days.
When I washed up on your shores I fell asleep,
and when I woke I saw your daughter playing
with her maids. I begged for her assistance
and she kindly gave me clothes from the laundry
and then directions how to find you.

ALCINOUS [*turning to his daughter*]:
Nausicaa, is this how I have raised you?
Your good judgment failed in this—
not to have brought him home directly
and have shown him the way!
Why did you make him come alone?

ODYSSEUS [*quickly*]:
My lord, you should not blame the princess.
She did tell me to come with her all the way,
but I would not. I felt ashamed beside her. All of us
on this earth are sometimes plagued with doubts.

ALCINOUS [*embarrassed*]:
Of course. How could I think—? We're all of us . . . Well . . .
Well, look to it then!

[*He addresses the* PHAECIANS.]

                    Get a black ship afloat
on the noble ocean, and pick our fastest sailor. Draft a crew
from among our younger men who have made a name at sea.
Loop oars well into your tholepins, lads, then leave the ship
and come straight back; back to the track and field.
I propose we should have competitions now,
so that when our guest is home among his friends
he might tell them what champions we are at javelin,
footracing, boxing, and wrestling. Who will compete?
Name off!

VARIOUS PHAECIANS [*severally*]:
Tideracer! Hullman! Sternman! Bluewater! Beacher!
Running Wake! Seabelt! Bordalee! Seareach!

ALCINOUS:
Our children all have seaside names.

[*Two* RACERS *take their marks.*]

Ready? Go!

[*They run off. Everyone is cheering. They reappear. One wins.*]

ALL:
Hurray for the winner! Hurray for the loser too!

48

[ALCINOUS, ARETE, *and* ODYSSEUS *stand aside, chatting.*]

LAODAMAS [*to his fellow* PHAECIANS]:
Look here, friends, we ought to ask the stranger
if he competes in something. He's no cripple,
and not old, though he may have gone stale under
the rough times he had.

SEAREACH:
You're right. Go up to him and ask.

ALCINOUS [*as* LAODAMAS *approaches*]:
This is one of my sons, Laodamas.

LAODAMAS:
Friend, Excellency, come join our competition,
if you are practiced, as you seem to be.
While a man lives he wins no greater honor
than racing and the skill that hands can bring him.

ODYSSEUS:
Laodamas, why do you challenge me?
I've more on my mind than track and field—
I've been on the sea for thirty-two days.
I'll watch, but I won't compete.

HULLMAN [*stepping forward*]:
The reason being, as I see it, friend,
you never learned a sport and have no skill
in any of the contests of fighting men.
You must have been the skipper of some tramp
that crawled from port to port looking for gold.

[*A long silence.*]

ODYSSEUS:
That was an ugly speech, friend. It's a shame
the gods don't give out more than one gift
at a time. You, for instance, are good-looking,
but your head is full of seashells. Give me that!

[*He takes* HULLMAN'*s javelin. He puts on a brave show, but he is not confident.* ATHENA *is beside him when he makes his throw, invisible to all. She takes the javelin as it leaves his hand and carries it high above her head and far away. After a long silence, we hear the javelin fall.* ATHENA *runs back on, appearing as a* YOUNG MAN.]

YOUNG MAN (ATHENA):
Friends! Even a blind man could judge this—
feeling with his fingers one spear, all alone, beyond the rest!

ODYSSEUS [*his blood up*]:
Come up to that one, lads,
I'll throw the next one farther!
Anyone else on edge for competition?
Inept at combat, am I? Not entirely!
Give me a smooth bow. I can handle it—
I hold myself the best hand with a bow.
What then, the discus? I'll plant it like an arrow!
Only in sprinting, I'm afraid, I may be passed
by someone. After *forty-seven days at sea*
my legs are weak. Who's next? Who's next?

ALCINOUS:
Friend, friend, we take no exception to what you say,
for this man has angered and affronted you
here at our peaceful games. You'd have us note
the prowess that is in you, and it is so clear
no man of sense would ever cry it down!
But listen to me now. Hear what matters to us.
When you are home with your wife and children
beside you, and talk turns to the Phaecians,
tell them this: we are fine at boxing and wrestling,
and we are first-rate runners and seamen,
but for all our days, the things in which we take the most delight
are feasting, music, the grace of dancing choirs,
having clean linen, hot baths, and our beds.

[*Everyone agrees.* ODYSSEUS *calms down.* ALCINOUS *addresses the* PHAECIANS.]

Let us all go on back to the palace
and present our guest with gifts: a piece
of cloth, or some jewel, or a bar of gold.
Then we shall have supper and entertainment.

PHAECIA: EVENING AND SINGING

ATHENA:
Now everyone was filled with joy. Alcinous
led the way and all went after, up to the palace,

[*Music. All the* PHAECIANS, ODYSSEUS, *and* ATHENA *travel back to the hall of the* PHAECIANS.]

They ate and drank until hunger and thirst were put aside.
But all grew still when someone new entered the great hall.

[DEMODOCUS *enters, led by the* MUSE, *who is invisible to all. Every-one quiets down.*]

ODYSSEUS:
Who is this?

ALCINOUS:
This is our singer, Demodocus. He knows
the good of life and evil—but she who gave him sweetness
also made him blind. Demodocus,
where is your Muse leading you? Let us hear.

DEMODOCUS:
Tonight, my lord, I feel within my heart
songs of the Acheans at Troy and,
above all, of Odysseus.

ODYSSEUS:
Sing only this for me. Sing this well,
and I shall say at once before the world
that it is by the grace of heaven we hear song
and music is the flower of life.

[*Music.* DEMODOCUS *sings.*]

DEMODOCUS:
Odysseus sailed in his black ship
to the land of the Trojans,

and he hid himself in a great horse,
and he conquered all the Trojans.
Twenty years he's not seen his home,
and Penelope lies there waiting.
How many days shall he wander on?
How many nights she'll be waiting.
How many nights—

[ODYSSEUS *is weeping.* ALCINOUS *stops the music.*]

ALCINOUS:
Hear me, lords and captains of Phaecia!
Let the singing stop; it isn't pleasing everybody.
Dear guest, since our poet began you've never
left off weeping. Now, you must not be
secretive any longer! Come, in fairness,
tell us your name. Tell us your native land—
we need sailing directions for our ships, you know.
Listen to me: I once heard my father say Poseidon
holds it against us that our deep sea ships
travel so fast and light upon the waves.
My father said someday one of our cutters,
homeward bound over the cloudy sea
after giving passage to a wayfarer,
would be wrecked by the gods, and a range of hills
thrown round our city. But even this old threat,
terrible as it is, has not forced us from our custom.
So you see, nothing you could say about yourself could
dissuade us. We will take you home.

[*Pause.*]

ODYSSEUS [quietly at first]:

> What shall I
say first? What shall I keep until the end?
The gods have tried me in a thousand ways.
I am Laertes' son, Odysseus.
My home is on the peaked seamark of Ithaca,
a rocky isle, but good for a boy's training;
I shall not see on earth a place more dear,
though I have been detained in the smooth caves
of Calypso, and in the halls of Circe the Enchantress.
Where shall a man find sweetness to surpass
his own home and his parents? In far lands
he shall not, though he find a house of gold.

But what of my sailing after Troy?

[Distant music. The MUSE crosses unseen to ODYSSEUS and embraces him. As he speaks, the PHAECIANS, ATHENA, and finally the MUSE disappear one by one. As they leave, they variously briefly embody fragmentary images of scenes ODYSSEUS describes before melting away.]

The wind that carried west from Ilion
brought me to Ismaros, on the far shore
a strongpoint on the coast of the Cicones.
I stormed that place and killed the men who fought.
Plunder, we took, equal shares to all—
but on the spot I told them: "Back, and quickly!
Out to sea again!" My men were mutinous,
fools, on stores of wine. Sheep after sheep
they butchered by the surf
and kept on feasting—while fugitives

went inland, calling to arms the main force of Cicones.
We made a fight of it,
backed on the ships, holding our beach,
although so far outnumbered,
but one by one we gave way.
Six benches were left empty in every ship
that evening when we pulled away from death.
And this new grief we bore with us to sea:
our precious lives we had, but not our friends.

[ODYSSEUS *is alone. Silence.*]

We put up our masts and let the breeze take over,
but as we came around Malea, the current took us out to sea.
Nine days we drifted. Upon the tenth, we came to
the land of the Lotus Eaters—

[*Music.*]

                                men who drowse all day
upon that flower. They have no will to do a person harm,
but those who taste this honeyed plant will forget
mother, child, and home and wish to stay forever
in the pleasure of the flower. Not knowing this, I
sent my men to explore, and soon enough, they
fell in with Lotus Eaters.

LOTUS EATERS

[*Music rises. The lovely, high, exotic* LOTUS EATERS *enter. They dance, smoke, kiss, and loll about. The air is perfumed; the light warm.* ODYSSEUS's SAILORS *enter, and one by one are seduced. The music is intoxicating.* ODYSSEUS *appears with other* SAILORS. *They manage to pry their shipmates from the arms of the* LOTUS EATERS, *but they continually slip back. Eventually,* ODYSSEUS *succeeds in getting them all away. A ship appears. The music ends.*]

I drove these men, wailing, back to the ships,
and called out to the rest:
                              All hands onboard;
come, clear the beach!
Filing in to their places by the rowlocks,
my oarsman dipped their long oars in the surf,
and we moved out again.

CYCLOPS

[*Slow, eerie music.* ODYSSEUS *joins his* SAILORS *on a ship.*]

                         After three days' hard rowing
it seemed we had drifted into a cloud upon the sea.
We could barely see our bows in the dense fog around us.
No lookout, nobody saw the island dead ahead:
we found ourselves in shallows, keels grazing shore.

[*The* SAILORS *disembark, turn their chairs over, and sleep against them.*]

We disembarked where the low ripples broke,
not knowing then that we had reached the land of Cyclopes.

[*Music ends.*]

SAILOR:
Captain, the men are all asleep. I—

ODYSSEUS:
I'll take first watch.
                    Now, Cyclopes
are giants, louts without a law to bless them.
They neither plow nor sow by hand,
they have no meetings, no consultation,
they dwell alone in lonely caves. And each one
has but one great eye in the middle of his forehead.
I did not know this then.

[*Dawn. The* SAILORS *stir.*]

                    Old shipmates, friends,
let's explore this land. Find out who the natives are—
for they may be wild savages, and lawless, or hospitable
and god-fearing men. Bring wine for an offering.

ATHENA [*in the heavens above*]:
Odysseus gave this last command because
in his bones he knew some towering brute
would be upon them soon—all outward power,
a wild man, ignorant of civility.

[ODYSSEUS *and his* SAILORS *approach the cave of the* CYCLOPS. SHEEP *are there in a pen.*]

ODYSSEUS:
We climbed a cliffside and crept inside a cave.
My men were uneasy.

SAILOR:

Captain, let's take these cheeses down to the ship,
then if there's time before the owner returns,
let's steal his sheep. If not, then let's straightaway
make for the open salt water.

ODYSSEUS:

                    No, I wish to meet the
owner of this cave. It's clear he's a shepherd
out tending his flocks.

[*As* ODYSSEUS *speaks, the* CYCLOPS *appears upstage, behind him. The*
SAILORS *see him and hear his approaching thunderous steps. (For*
additional staging suggestions, see the appendix, page 171.)]

               I have hopes, men,
that we might collect some friendly gifts
from him. The gods will smile on us, and . . .
men? Men?

CYCLOPS [*bellowing*]:

Strangers, who are you? What are you doing
in my home? Are you wandering rogues, who
cast your lives like dice and ravage other folk by sea?

ODYSSEUS:

We are Acheans, homeward bound from Troy.
Sir, do not harm us! Zeus will avenge the unoffending guest.

CYCLOPS:

Little man, you must come from the other end
of nowhere, telling me to mind the gods. We Cyclopes

are stronger than the gods. Who cares for them?
But tell me, where was it, now, that you have moored
your ship? Around the point, or down the shore, I wonder?

ODYSSEUS:
My ship? Poseidon broke it up on the rocks at your
land's end. We are survivors, these good men and I.

CYCLOPS:
Come here, why don't you, so I might take a closer look.

[*Two foolish* SAILORS *approach.*]

ODYSSEUS:
Don't go. Stay back! Stay back!

OTHER SAILORS [*simultaneously*]:
No, do as he says! Do as he says!

[*The* CYCLOPS *grabs the two, tears them to pieces, and devours them.*]

CYCLOPS:
That was good. You Acheans make a fine meal.

ODYSSEUS:
With that, the Cyclops drew a boulder
in front of the cave's mouth and fell asleep.

SAILOR:
Odysseus! Now's our chance! Take your spear and stab him!

ODYSSEUS:
Don't you understand? If we kill him now,
we'll never leave this cave. All of us together
can never push that boulder aside.

ATHENA:
All that night, he prayed to Athena to grant him
some idea. In the morning, the Cyclops stirred,
grabbed two more men for breakfast, and departed
with his sheep, rolling the boulder back in place.

[*The* CYCLOPS *exits.*]

SAILOR:
Odysseus! Do something!

ODYSSEUS:
                              Men, take this olive branch
and scrape it down. Cut off a six-foot section
and make a stake with a pointed end.

ATHENA:
All day long they held the stake in the fire's heart
and turned it, toughening it, then hid it, well back
in the cavern, under one of the dung piles in profusion there.
At evening came the shepherd with his woolly flock.

[*The* CYCLOPS *enters, blocks the cave with a boulder, and sits to milk his* SHEEP.]

ODYSSEUS:

                                        Cyclops, try some wine.
Here's liquor to wash down your scraps of men.
Taste it, and see the kind of drink we carry
under our planks. I meant it for an offering
if you would help us home.

CYCLOPS:

Give me another, thank you kindly. Tell me,
how are you called? I'll make a gift will please you.

ODYSSEUS:

Cyclops, you ask my honorable name? Remember
the gift you promised me, and I shall tell you.
My name is Nobody: mother, father, and friends,
everyone calls me Nobody.

[*The* SAILORS *concur, repeating* "Nobody." *Even the* SHEEP *say* "No-baaady."]

CYCLOPS:

Nobody, here's your gift:
I'll eat you last after all your friends.

[*The* CYCLOPS *laughs, then passes out.*]

ODYSSEUS:

Men, this is our chance. May the gods help us!

ATHENA:

Forward they sprinted, lifted the olive branch,
and rammed it deep in his crater eye. Eyelid

and lash were seared; the pierced ball hissed,
and the roots popped.

CYCLOPS:
Cyclopes! Cyclopes! Help me! Help!

[FIRST NEIGHBORING CYCLOPS *and* SECOND NEIGHBORING CYCLOPS
appear.]

FIRST NEIGHBORING CYCLOPS:
                             What ails you,
Polyphemos? Why do you cry so sore
in the starry night, depriving us of sleep?

SECOND NEIGHBORING CYCLOPS:
Is a robber stealing away your sheep,
is somebody trying to kill you or ruin you?

CYCLOPS:
Nobody! Nobody's tricked me! Nobody's ruined me!

FIRST NEIGHBORING CYCLOPS:
Ah well, if nobody has played you foul
there in your lonely bed, you must be sick.

CYCLOPS:
But Nobody—!

SECOND NEIGHBORING CYCLOPS:
Sickness comes from Zeus and can't be helped.

FIRST NEIGHBORING CYCLOPS:
Pray to your father, Lord Poseidon.

[FIRST NEIGHBORING CYCLOPS *and* SECOND NEIGHBORING CYCLOPS
depart. ODYSSEUS *laughs and laughs.*]

ATHENA:
Odysseus was filled with laughter
to see how like a charm the trick had worked.

[CYCLOPS *blocks the entrance to the cave with his body.*]

SAILOR ONE:
What now, Odysseus? We can't run past him!

SAILOR TWO:
We're finished! Odysseus!

ODYSSEUS:
What? You think that idiot can defeat me?
I have another trick. Death sits there huge,
but my wits are greater.

ATHENA:
Odysseus took the woolly sheep from their pens
and tied them together in groups of three.
Then underneath each group he secured a man.

CYCLOPS:
Poor sheep, it's time for you to go; go on—
out to the lush green pastures.

ATHENA:
Blinded, sick with pain, the master stroked
each fleecy back, then let it pass. He never
felt the men below, their fingers twirled
deep in sheepskin ringlets for an iron grip.

[*All the* SAILORS *have escaped.*]

ODYSSEUS:
Last of all, my ram, the leader, came,
weighted by wool and me with my meditations.

CYCLOPS [*gently*]:
Sweet cousin ram, why lag behind the rest
in the night cave? You never linger so,
but graze before them all, and go afar
to crop sweet grass and take your stately way
leading along the streams, until at evening
you run to be the first one in the fold.
Why now so far behind? Can you be grieving
over your master's eye? That carrion rogue
and his accursed companions burned it out
when he had conquered all my wits with wine.
Nobody will get out alive, I swear.

[*His rage grows.*]

Oh, had you brain and voice to tell
where he may be now, dodging all my fury!
Bashed by this hand and bashed on this rock wall
his brains would strew across the floor,
for the outrage Nobody worked on me!

[*The ram passes by with* ODYSSEUS *beneath.*]

ODYSSEUS:
We took the Cyclops's precious sheep and ran
down to the shore.

[*Drumming. They run to the ship and begin to row furiously.* ATHENA
comes down and places a little boat in front of the blinded CYCLOPS
and pulls it slowly away from him on a string.]

We loaded up the ships
and set to sail. I shouted to my adversary:
O Cyclops! Would you feast on my companions?

CYCLOPS [*blindly lunging at the little boat*]:
Nobody?

ODYSSEUS:
Puny, am I, in a caveman's hands?

SAILOR ONE:
Godsake, Captain! Why bait the beast again?
Let him alone!

CYCLOPS:
Nobody? Nobody!

[*The* CYCLOPS *gropes at a boulder.*]

ODYSSEUS:
How do you like what we've done to you?

SAILOR TWO:
Captain!

ODYSSEUS:
You damned cannibal!

SAILOR THREE:
You're giving him bearing with your shouting!

SAILOR FOUR:
He'll smash our timbers and our heads together!

ODYSSEUS:
But in my glorying spirit, I would not heed them.
I let my anger flare and yelled:
                              Cyclops!
If ever mortal man inquire
how you were put to shame and blinded, tell him
Odysseus, raider of cities, took your eye:
Laertes' son, who lives on Ithaca.

[CYCLOPS *stops, the boulder above his head.*]

CYCLOPS:
Odysseus? It was foretold to me that one day
I would lose my great eye at Odysseus's hands.
I had in mind some giant, armed in giant force.
But this, but you—small, pitiful, and twiggy—

[*He drops to the ground and struggles toward the little boat.*
ATHENA *pulls it safely out of reach.*]

come back, Odysseus, and I'll treat you well,
praying to Poseidon to treat you well. I am his son.
He may heal me of this wound.

ODYSSEUS:
If I could take your life I would and take
your time away and hurl you down to hell!
Poseidon could not heal you there!

[POSEIDON *enters upstage with his triton.*]

CYCLOPS [*kneeling and praying to the sky*]:
Oh, hear me, Father, Lord Poseidon,
grant that Odysseus never see his home!
Should destiny intend he see his roof again,
far be that day and dark the years between.
Let him lose all companions and return
under strange sail to bitter days at home.

[*The drumming and the rowing stop.*]

ODYSSEUS:
In these words he prayed.

POSEIDON AND ODYSSEUS:
And the god heard him.

ODYSSEUS:
This is why I have not seen my home, my wife,
my son, in all these years: I blinded this
monster's only eye, and then I said my name.

[*Silence, then the* CYCLOPS, POSEIDON, *and* ATHENA *exit.*]

AEOLUS

ODYSSEUS:
After a hard day's rowing, we made our
next landfall on the floating island of Aeolia,
domain of Aeolus Hippotades, king of the winds
both mild and violent.

[AEOLUS *enters with his family. The* SAILORS *disembark, and the boat disappears.*]

Now I must tell you, this king has twelve
children—six daughters and six lusty sons—
and he gave girls to boys to be their gentle brides.
Here we put in, while Aeolus played host to me.
He kept me one full month to hear the tale of Troy.
When it was time for us to leave, I asked for his help.

AEOLUS:
Odysseus, in exchange for all your tale of Troy
we'll stint at nothing. We'll give you provisions,
and here—

[*A* SERVANT *enters with a giant bag.*]

　　　　here are all our boisterous
storm winds sewn up in a bag. Wedge it under
your afterdeck, secure it with burnished wire

to prevent the slightest leakage, and you shall
have fair passage home.

[*A boat with four* SAILORS *appears.* ODYSSEUS *boards.* AEOLUS *turns
his back but remains onstage. His family leaves.*]

ODYSSEUS:
Then he called up a breeze from the west
to send us on our way. For nine days we sailed
without incident, I manned the till alone,
and on the tenth—

SAILOR:
Ithaca!

ODYSSEUS:
Ithaca, our homeland, came in sight.
Men, I find I'm weary to the bone, bring
the ship . . . on . . . home.

[*He falls asleep.*]

SAILORS [*variously*]:
Sleep well, Odysseus.
Yes, Odysseus.
Don't worry.

[*Things grow quiet. During the following,* ATHENA *enters and walks
slowly across the stage, upstage of the* SAILORS, *carrying a small
boat before her in her hands. The* SAILORS *row in silence for a while.*]

SAILOR ONE [*casually*]:
What do you suppose is in the bag?

SAILOR TWO:
Presents from Aeolus. Silver, I think. And gold.

SAILOR THREE:
It never fails. He's welcomed everywhere:
Hail to the captain, have some gifts.

[*They row in silence.*]

SAILOR FOUR:
What did you all get from Troy?

SAILOR ONE:
Nothing.

SAILOR THREE:
Nothing.

SAILOR TWO:
I got this.

[*He holds up a little souvenir from Troy. Nothing much. The* SAILORS *stop rowing for a moment to look, then begin to row again in silence.*]

SAILOR ONE:
Odysseus got a lot at Troy.

SAILOR FOUR:
Well, he is the captain.

SAILOR ONE:
True.

[*They row.*]

SAILOR THREE [*suddenly*]:
Let's see what's in the bag.

[*They dash to the back of the boat and open the bag of winds.*]

SAILOR ONE:
I can't see anyth—

[*An enormous storm comes up. The little ship flies out of* ATHENA's *hands. The chairs topple; the* SAILORS *roll around. Ithaca disappears from view.*]

SAILORS:
Ithaca!

ODYSSEUS [*waking*]:
Men! What have you done!

SAILORS:
Ithaca! Ithaca!

ODYSSEUS:
       Every wind
roared into hurricane; the ships went pitching

west; our land was lost. The rough gale blew the ships
and rueful crews clear back to Aeolia.

[*The boat is reassembled. The* SAILORS *are embarrassed.*]

AEOLUS:
Why back again, Odysseus? What sea fiend
rose in your path? Didn't we launch you
well for home, or whatever land you chose?

ODYSSEUS:
It was my rascally crew, and a fatal nap.
Make good my loss, dear friend!

[AEOLUS *is suddenly, irrationally furious. He storms.*]

AEOLUS:
Get out of here! The world holds no more
creeping thing than you, Odysseus! Out!
Your voyage is cursed by heaven!

ODYSSEUS:
He drove me from the place, groan as I would,
and comfortless we went again to sea, no breeze
to help us on our way: six indistinguishable
days and nights. At last we made landfall
on the island of Aiaia.

CIRCE

[*Strange music. The* SAILORS *disembark, and the boat disappears as they exit.*]

ODYSSEUS:
                Some god must have guided
us in, for we came into a cove without a sound.
I climbed a rocky point and saw a wisp of
smoke from some woodland hall. I sent half
my men off to explore, but late that day
only one returned.

[*Music ends.* EURYLOCHUS *runs on, terrified.*]

EURYLOCHUS:
Odysseus, glory of commanders, our
friends are lost—are gone!

ODYSSEUS:
Speak, Eurylochus, what happened?

[*As* EURYLOCHUS *speaks, the* SAILORS *enter upstage and approach* CIRCE's *palace. There are* ENCHANTED ANIMALS *there. All transpires as* EURYLOCHUS *describes.*]

EURYLOCHUS:
We went up through the forest where you sent us
until we found a palace, in a glade,
a marvelous stone house on open ground.
In the entrance lay wolves and mountain lions,
animals of all kinds—but none attacked.

Oh—it was strange, I tell you—
they fawned on us with their mighty paws;
they switched their long tails like hounds
who look up when their master comes, or lie
beneath a table.

ODYSSEUS:
What next?

[CIRCE *enters.*]

EURYLOCHUS:
There was a woman inside; she called to us.

CIRCE:
Welcome, dear strangers—sailors by your looks—
come in! Come in, poor tired men.

ODYSSEUS:
They didn't.

EURYLOCHUS:
They did! They followed her like sheep! Only I
was afraid, and hid outside by the entrance.

CIRCE:
Oh, you big, poor, sad, tired, tired, big poor men!
What hard work, rowing those big, big ships! That
must be so hard!

SAILORS [*variously*]:
Yes . . . yes . . . it is . . .

74

CIRCE:
However do you do it? All day long? Drink up.

[*She offers them drinks in golden goblets.*]

SAILORS [*variously*]:
Thank you, thank you, kind lady. . . .

SAILOR ONE [*toasting*]:
Dear lady, we salute you. You are the essence
of hospitality. Even your animals are kind,
they seem almost hu—, almost hum—

[*He begins to snort and grunt. The others do the same. They all turn
into swine—unhappy, distressed swine.*]

CIRCE:
What's that? What's that you're trying to say?
Speak up, dear. What's the matter? Cat got
your tongue? Sooooo-eeee! Sooooo-eeee! Sooooo-eeee!

[*She laughs, herds the* PIGS *around, then strolls off. The* PIGS *remain,
disconsolate.*]

EURYLOCHUS:
None of our friends came out of that house.
I waited for hours; only swine filled the yard!

ODYSSEUS:
Take me back the way you came.

EURYLOCHUS:
Not back there, O my lord! Oh, leave me here!

ODYSSEUS:
By heaven, Eurylochus, rest here then, but
let me go; I see nothing for it but to go.

[EURYLOCHUS *runs off.* HERMES *enters from above.*]

I turned and left him to find the subtle witch,
but Hermes met me, with his golden wand.

HERMES:
Odysseus, what do you think you're doing?
Wandering all alone on this strange island?
Your friends are turned to pigs in Circe's house
and you will be too if you don't listen.

ODYSSEUS:
What should I do?

HERMES:
Her charm is in her golden Pramian wine.
Take this; it's an antidote. When she sees you
are impervious to her spell, she'll want to go to bed.
I advise you to do it.

[HERMES *departs.* ODYSSEUS *drinks the antidote, then continues on his journey.*]

ODYSSEUS:
Through the island trees I sought out Circe,
my heart high with excitement, beating hard.

[*He is surrounded by the pleading, inarticulate* PIGS.]

CIRCE [*entering with wine*]:
Welcome, dear stranger. Welcome to my home!
Come in, come in, don't mind the swine.

ODYSSEUS:
Why, thank you.

CIRCE:
May I offer you some golden Pramian wine?

[*The* PIGS *squeal in warning.*]

ODYSSEUS:
Thank you very kindly.

CIRCE:
Drink up.

ODYSSEUS:
I will.

[ODYSSEUS *drinks the wine.*]

CIRCE:
Down in the sty and snore among the rest!

[*Nothing happens.*]

CIRCE:
I said, Down in the sty and snore among the rest!

[*Nothing happens.* CIRCE *turns to run.* ODYSSEUS *grabs her and puts his dagger to her throat.*]

ODYSSEUS:
Release my men this instant from your charms
or I will cut this fair throat of yours!

CIRCE:
How did you resist my spell? You can't be
mortal! Zeus will not approve of one god
behaving this way to another!

ODYSSEUS:
                              I assure you, lady,
I am human, as human as my men,
or as they will be when you release them—

CIRCE:
Odysseus?

[ODYSSEUS *is startled to be called by name.*]

I was told one day you'd come to visit me;
Hermes said your black ship would bring you here.
Put up your sword, put your weapon
in its sheath. O great contender, we two

shall mingle and make love upon our bed,
so that in love and sleep, we learn to trust—

ODYSSEUS:
O Circe, would you make me soft and doting now,
when here in this house you turned my men to swine?
I'll mount no bed of love with you upon it—
or, if I do, swear me first a great oath,
you'll restore my men, and work
no more enchantment to our harm.

CIRCE:
I swear.

[*Music. They embrace. The* PIGS *become* SAILORS *again and wander off.* ODYSSEUS *pulls away. Music ends.*]

Son of Laertes, master mariner, enough of weeping fits!
Your cruel wandering is all you think of, never of joy,
after so many blows. Stay here and rest, Odysseus.

ODYSSEUS:
I could not help consenting.
So day by day we lingered, until a year grew fat.
But in the pause of summer, my shipmates
summoned me and said:

SAILOR [*entering*]:
Captain, shake off this trance and think of home.

[*The* SAILOR *exits.* ODYSSEUS *takes* CIRCE *by the knees.*]

CIRCE:
Son of Laertes, master mariner, you shall not stay
against your will. But listen to me now:
you will never come to see your hall on Ithaca
unless you take a strange way round.

ODYSSEUS:
What way is that?

CIRCE:
You must go down to the cold and crumbling home of
Death and Pale Persephone, down to the Underworld.
There the flitting ghost of blind Teiresias has prophecy for you.

[*Music.* CIRCE *exits.*]

ODYSSEUS:
So Circe spoke, and my heart felt like a stone.
I woke my men, told them the sorry news.
But I was not to take all my men unharmed
even from Circe's mild island. Among them all
the youngest was Elpenor—

[*As* ODYSSEUS *speaks,* ELPENOR *appears, walking sleepily. Behind
him, all the* PHAECIANS, *the* MUSE, *and* ATHENA, *one by one, return
and move into the places they had when* ODYSSEUS *first began to tell
his tale.*]

no mainstay in a fight nor very clever—
and this one, having climbed on Circe's roof
to taste the cool night, fell asleep with wine.

Waked by our morning voices, he started up,
but missed his footing on the long steep backward ladder

[ELPENOR *stumbles.*]

and fell that height headlong. His neck was broken
and his ghost fled to the dark. But I was outside,
walking with my friends.

[*As* ELPENOR *falls, he rolls into place as a* PHAECIAN, *and the return to the Phaecian palace is complete.*]

ALCINOUS:
Odysseus, why have you stopped? You seem
so grieved. Please, tell us: Did you in truth
go down into the Underworld?
Whom did you meet among the dead?

ODYSSEUS:
Alcinous, king and admiration of men, there is a time
for storytelling, and there is a time for rest.

ALCINOUS:
Forgive us, dear Odysseus, you are right.
We will resume after we have rested.

[*Music. As* ATHENA *speaks, each member of the company stands, walks slowly upstage, lies down on the foor, and turns in sleep.*]

ATHENA:
So the good Odysseus, after all his troubles, sleeps
in the echoing portico, while Alcinous lies down
for the night with Arete, who makes and shares his bed.

[*Music ends.*]

ACT II

THE UNDERWORLD

[*The act begins with the* PHAECIANS *in their former positions, listening to* ODYSSEUS. *The* MUSE *is with him.*]

ODYSSEUS:
Lord Alcinous, king and admiration of men,
you have promised me safe passage home,
and if indeed listening is still your pleasure,
I must not grudge my part: I will go on.

[*Music. During the following,* ODYSSEUS *comes forward. The* PHAE-
CIANS *and the* MUSE *drift away. As they leave, they variously embody fragmentary images—the ship launchings, the men of winter,
etc.—before disappearing entirely.*]

We launched our ship on the fathomless unresting sea.
By night we ran toward the ocean's edge,
past where the Men of Winter live, hidden

in mist and cloud. We made the land and took our way
along the River of Ocean to the spot foretold by Circe.
There, I dug a pit and poured in the blood of a
black lamb. The spirits all came swarming up to drink,
their eager faces flickering in the dark.
The last to die was the first to greet me:
and this is how I, a living man, went into the Underworld.

[*The music changes.* ELPENOR *appears, and another figure is crouching in the distance.* ELPENOR *speaks about himself calmly, as from a great distance of time. (For additional staging suggestions, see the appendix, page 171.)*]

ELPENOR:
I slept on Circe's roof, then could not see
the long steep backward ladder, coming down,
and fell that height. My neck bone buckled under,
snapped, and my spirit found this well of dark.
Now hear the grace I pray for, in the name
of those back in the world, not here—your wife
and father, he who gave you bread in childhood,
and your own child, your only son, Telemachus,
long ago left at home.
              When you make sail
you will moor ship, I know, on Circe's island;
there, O my lord, remember me, I pray,
do not abandon me, unwept, unburied,
to tempt the gods' wrath while you sail for home;
but fire my corpse, and all the gear I had,
and build a tomb for me above the breakers—
an unknown sailor's mark for men to come.

Heap up the mound there, and plant upon it
the oar I pulled in life with my companions.

[ELPENOR *disappears.* TEIRESIAS *enters.*]

ODYSSEUS:

Now when I saw him
there, I knew we had left him, unwept, unburied,
and I cried for pity and called out to him—but
his faint, unhappy image left me as another rose
to take his place: this was Teiresias, whom Circe
foretold would give me prophecy.

TEIRESIAS:

Great Captain,
a fair wind and the honey lights of home
are all you seek. But anguish lies ahead: you will
make landfall on Thrinacia, the island of Helios,
the sun. There you'll find his gentle grazing herds.
Hear this: If your shipmates lay a hand on them,
I see destruction for them all. You will survive,
but alone and lost for years.

Now, when you
are home, take an oar upon your shoulder and walk
so far inland that you find men who have
never seen the sea, nor known its tides nor waves,
nor seen seagoing ships that glory in the wind.
One day, a passerby will ask about the oar, saying,
"What is that on your shoulder, a winnowing fan?"
At that moment stop and plant the oar in the ground.
Then make sacrifice to Lord Poseidon.

Do this,
And a seaborne death, soft as this hand of mist,
will come upon you when you are wearied out
with rich old age, your country folk in blessed peace
around you. And all this shall be just as I foretell.

[TEIRESIAS *departs.*]

ODYSSEUS:
When he had prophesied, Teiresias's shade
retired lordly to the halls of Death;
but then I saw a figure, crouching in the gloom,
and when she turned I saw it was my mother.

[*The* COUCHING FIGURE *turns and rises.*]

ODYSSEUS'S MOTHER:
Odysseus?

ODYSSEUS:
Mother, is that you? Are you alone,
or is Father here as well, or Penelope?
Is she here, or is she still at home?

ODYSSEUS'S MOTHER:
Still with your child she is, poor heart,
still in your palace hall. Forlorn her nights
and days go by, her life used up in weeping.
But no man takes your honored place.

ODYSSEUS:
And Father, what of him?

ODYSSEUS'S MOTHER:
                         Old Laertes
is country bound and comes to town no more.
He owns no bedding, rugs, or fleecy mantles,
but lies down, winter nights, among the shepherds,
rolled in old cloaks for cover near the embers.
Or when the heat comes at the end of summer,
with fallen leaves he makes his lowly bed.
He lies there even now, with aching heart,
longing for your return while age comes on him.
So I, too, pined away, so death befell me,
not that illness overtook me—no true illness:
only my loneliness for you, Odysseus,
for your kind heart and counsel, gentle Odysseus,
took my life away.

ODYSSEUS:
I rose and tried three times to embrace her,
but she went sifting through my arms, impalpable
as shadows are, and wavering like a dream.

                              O my mother,
will you not stay, be still, here in my arms,
may we not, even in this place of Death,
hold each other and touch with love?

ODYSSEUS'S MOTHER:
                         Go now, my child,
you must be craving sunlight.

[*Exit* ODYSSEUS'S MOTHER. *In an instant, the music stops, and the lights come up very bright. No shadows remain.* ODYSSEUS *is alone on a barren stage.* ALCINOUS *enters quietly.*]

ALCINOUS:
Son of Laertes, I have pressed you to go on, but this—

ODYSSEUS:
Alcinous—

ALCINOUS:
Perhaps some things should not be told—

ODYSSEUS:
King Alcinous, you pressed me to go on,
and now I must. Let me conclude my tale.

My crew and I returned to Aiaia, Circe's island.
I sent my shipmates to bring Elpenor's body
from the house of Circe and gave him the rights
of burial as he begged me in the Underworld.

ELPENOR'S FUNERAL AND CIRCE'S INSTRUCTIONS

[*Music.* ALCINOUS *exits as a small funeral procession of* SAILORS *enters with the body of* ELPENOR. CIRCE *follows behind. As she speaks, the* SAILORS *plant the oar of* ELPENOR *where they bury him.*]

CIRCE:
                                        So, son of Laertes,
You went down alive to the house of Death?

Most men are satisfied to die just once,
but you will do so twice. Come along:
listen to what I say.
                        Square in your ship's path
are Sirens, singing to bewitch men coasting by—
woe to the innocent who hears that sound!—
He will never see his home or lady again;
the Sirens will lure his mind away. Bones
of dead men are rotting in a pile beside them.

ODYSSEUS:
Might I not contrive a way to hear that song,
and yet escape the danger?

CIRCE:
Plug your oarsmen's ears with beeswax,
and have them bind you to the mast.
Shout as you will to be untied, your crew
must only twist more line around you
until the singer's voices fade.

ODYSSEUS:
What then?

CIRCE:
One of two courses you must take,
and you yourself must weigh them.
You will pass between Scylla and Charybdis.
Scylla is a monster with twelve arms and six heads.
She takes from every ship that passes her
one man for each mouth. Yet if you steer wide

of her, you'll meet the whirlpool,
Charybdis. She can take your whole ship down.

ODYSSEUS:
Only instruct me, Goddess, how I may pass Charybdis,
or fight off Scylla when she tries to raid my crew?

CIRCE:
There is no fighting her. Give in to her!
Better to mourn six men than lose
your whole ship.

ODYSSEUS:
                O Goddess—

CIRCE:
                                Enough!
Now, tell me, what did you learn
from the blind Teiresias? What did he forecast?

ODYSSEUS:
A strange thing: he said if ever I reach home,
I must, when I am old, take an oar and walk
so far inland I find a place where men
have never seen the sea, and at that spot
plant the oar, if I wish a peaceful death.

CIRCE:
Heed him, Odysseus, and all will be
as he foretold.
                Farewell, Son of Laertes.
Remember me.

[CIRCE *leaves.*]

SIRENS

ODYSSEUS:
I made straight for the ship and roused the men.
They scrambled to their places by the rowlocks.
We pulled away from Circe's island, but soon enough
the wind fell, and a calm came over all the sea.

Plug up your ears and tie me down!
The Sirens have begun!

[*The* SIRENS *enter: a* NURSE, GIRL SCOUT, BUSINESSWOMAN, TEACHER, BRIDE, *and* NUN, *all clothed entirely in red. They bring chairs with them and sit down. One* SIREN *gives a note on a pitch pipe, but the text is spoken in unison, not sung.*]

SIRENS [*in unison, seductively, with pauses between each phrase*]:
Everything. You do. Is so. Important.

[*Together, but variously.*]

Oh, you big, big sad poor tired tired men. You big sad poor tired tired men! Oh you big, big, sad poor tired tired men, you big sad poor tired tired men!

[*Together again.*]

Everything. You say. Just fills. Me up.

My face, my face, is nothing but a mirror,
my arms, my arms, are nothing but a cradle,
my self, my self, is nothing.

ONE SIREN:
This way, oh, turn your bows,
Glory of Achea,
as all the world allows—
moor and be merry.

OTHER SIRENS:
My face, my face, is nothing but a mirror.

ONE SIREN:
Sweet coupled airs we sing.
No lonely seafarer
holds clear of entering
our green mirror.

OTHER SIRENS:
My arms, my arms, are nothing but a cradle.

ONE SIREN:
Pleased by each purring note
like honey twining
from her throat and my throat,
who lies a-pining?

SIRENS [*all, in unison*]:
My face my face is nothing but a mirror,
my arms, my arms, are nothing but a cradle.
my self, my self, is nothing.

TEACHER SIREN [*reading from a thesaurus*]:
Woman, definition: noun, woman, she, female, petticoat, skirt, moll,
broad,

OTHER SIRENS:
Your life. Is bigger. Than mine.

TEACHER SIREN [*continuing*]:
feminality, femininity, feminine, womanhood, etc., feminism; gyne-
cology, gyniatrics, gynics.

OTHER SIRENS:
You're perfect the way you are. Don't change.

TEACHER SIREN [*continuing*]:
Womankind; the fair sex, softer sex; the distaff side, weaker vessel,
dame, madam, madame, mistress,

OTHER SIRENS:
I love it when you ignore me.

TEACHER SIREN [*continuing*]:
Mrs., lady, memsahib, Frau, señora, signora, donna, belle, matron,
dowager, goody gammer; good-woman, goodwife, squaw, wife, etc.,
matronhood, matronage,

[*The* SIRENS *all begin to speak in unison. They leave their chairs, move provocatively, use their chairs provocatively, although their tone may be straightforward, almost businesslike.*]

SIRENS:

venus, nymph, wench, grisette, little bit of fluff, girl, etc., inamorata, love, etc., courtesan, etc., spinster, virgin, bachelor girl, new woman, amazon; see also *girl.* Girl, noun, (1) a young unmarried female person; i.e.: "hired a girl to babysit," synonyms: damsel, gal, lass, lassie, maid, maiden, miss, missy, quail, quiff, wench, tomboy, deb, debutante, subdeb, subdebutante, bobbysoxer, schoolgirl, gamin, (2) synonyms: see *maid* 2. 3, syn.; see *girlfriend.*

[*The* SIRENS *pick up their chairs and leave, speaking casually over their shoulders as they go.*]

No, don't get up; I'll take care of it.
No, don't get up; I'll take care of it.
No, don't get up; I'll take care of it.

[*The* SIRENS *fade away.*]

SCYLLA

ODYSSEUS:

My faithful company
rowed past the Sirens until they dropped
under the rim of the sea, and their singing
dwindled away. The crew rested on their oars,

peeling off the wax that I had laid thick
on their ears, then set me free.

But scarcely had that island
faded in blue air than I saw smoke
and white water, with a sound of waves
in tumult—a sound the men heard,
and it terrified them. I knew we were now
upon the strait between the terrible whirlpool
of Charybdis and the sea monster Scylla.

SAILOR ONE:
What now, Captain?

SAILOR TWO:
What did Circe tell you?

SAILOR THREE:
What lies ahead?

ODYSSEUS:
                Heads up, lads!
We must obey the orders as I give them.
Get the oarshafts in your hands and lay back
hard on your benches: hit these breaking seas.
Drive far away from the whirlpool; head
toward the cliff on the other side.

SAILOR TWO:
Is that what Circe said to do?

SAILOR FOUR:
Is that all she said?

ODYSSEUS:
Yes, yes, my friends, that's all she said.

I told them nothing, as they could do nothing.
They would have dropped their oars in panic
to roll for cover under the decking, and we all
would have been lost.

Row hard, men, toward the cliff!

[SCYLLA *slowly rises up behind the boat.*]

PERIMEDES [*a* SAILOR]:
Captain, speak to me, tell me something now
to calm me down. My heart is clamoring, I don't
know why. Captain, help me. Speak to me.

[SCYLLA *is creeping up behind* PERIMEDES. ODYSSEUS *sees this.*]

ODYSSEUS:
Look at me, Perimedes, look here, my friend.
Have we never been in danger before this?

[PERIMEDES *starts to turn around.*]

Look at me—is this worse than when the Cyclops
penned us in his cave? What power he had! How
huge he was—but didn't I keep my nerve and use

my wits to save you then? Look here. Look at me.
Look at me—

[SCYLLA *overtakes and devours* PERIMEDES.]

Six men were borne aloft in spasms toward the cliff,
still reaching for me. Deathly pity ran through me
at the sight of that—the worst I ever suffered
questing the strange passes of the sea.

THE ISLAND OF THE SUN AND CHARYBDIS

ODYSSEUS:
On we went, in despair, the men exhausted
at their oars. But soon we came near the coast
of the noble island of Helios, where grazed
those cattle with wide brows and bounteous flocks.
From the black ship, far still at sea, I heard
the lowing of the cattle winding home
and sheep bleating, and heard, too, in my heart
the words of blind Teiresias and Circe
who forbade me the island of Helios.

Shipmates, grieving and weary though you are,
listen: I had forewarning we must shun
this island of the Sun. Pull away, then,
and put the land astern.

SAILOR ONE:
Are you flesh and blood, Odysseus,
to endure more than a man?

SAILOR TWO:
Do you never tire?

SAILOR ONE:
God, look at you, iron is what you're made of.

SAILOR THREE:
Here we all are, half dead with rowing—

SAILOR FOUR:
Falling asleep at the oars

SAILOR THREE:
And you say no landing, no firm earth
where we could make a quiet supper.

SAILOR FIVE:
No, you say pull out to sea—

SAILOR SIX:
With night upon us!

SAILOR FIVE:
Just as before, but wandering now, and lost!

SAILOR SIX:
Sudden storms can rise at night
and swamp ships without a trace!

ODYSSEUS:
I see I am alone, outmatched.
Let this whole company swear me a great oath:

any herd of cattle or flock of sheep we find
shall go unharmed. Do you swear?

[*The* SAILORS *swear.*]

All hands ashore!
                    We meant to stay
the night. But Poseidon had not forgotten me.
He turned the sea to glass. Not one breeze
to trouble that green mirror. We could
not launch; and so for a month we lingered
where we never should have come. Day in,
day out, we burned on that island. Our bread
and wine were gone. The men began to roam
the wild shore, lean days wore their bellies thin.

                                        Men, I must go
to the interior, pray to the gods in solitude
and offer sacrifice. Remember your oath to me.

SAILORS [*variously*]:
Yes, Captain. . . . We will, Captain. . . . Yes, Odysseus. . . .

[ODYSSEUS *leaves. There is a sound like the ticking of a clock. The
men sit around, bored, playing little games, growing irritable in
their hunger, beginning to tussle with each other. A* SHEEP *enters.
She circles innocently through and around the* SAILORS. *They try to
ignore her, but slowly, without speaking, they form a barrier to trap
her. They kill her. The sky darkens, and some of the* SAILORS *seem
transformed into slaughtered cattle, strangely lowing while roast-
ing on the spit.* ODYSSEUS *returns.*]

ODYSSEUS:

When I came down the seaward path, the savory
odors of burnt fat eddied around me.
Grief took hold of me. The silken herd was dead.
The gods made strange signs appear:
cowhides began to crawl, and beef, both raw
and roasted, lowed as though alive upon the spits.
All the gales had ceased, we launched into the sea.
We held our course but briefly. Then the squall
struck, whining from the west, with gale force.
With crack on crack of thunder, Zeus let fly
a bolt against the ship, a direct hit,
and all the men were flung into the waves.

                                  No more seafaring

homeward for these, no sweet day of return;
the god had turned his face from them.

[*All* SAILORS *exit.* ODYSSEUS *is alone.*]

I clambered onto a single timber, and all that night
I drifted. Sure enough, in the sunrise, I lay
off Scylla mountain and Charybdis deep.
There, as the whirlpool drank the tide, a billow
tossed me, and I sprang for a great fig tree,
catching on like a bat under a bough.
And ah! How long, with what desire, I waited!
Till, at the twilight hour, the long pole
at last reared from the sea.

[*As he continues, the* PHAECIANS, ATHENA, *and the* MUSE *enter one by one.*]

Now I let go with hands and feet, plunging
straight into the foam and pulled astride.
I drifted nine days in the open sea
before I made shore upon Calypso's island.
She received me, loved me. Eight years she kept me
as her heart's delight; but in my heart I never
gave consent. At last she released me, and
the currents brought me here to you.

[*The* PHAECIANS, ATHENA, *and the* MUSE *are in their original positions, listening to* ODYSSEUS.]

DEPARTURE FROM PHAECIA

ALCINOUS:

                              Odysseus,
however painful all the past, you'll have
clear sailing now. You came under
my tall roof, begging for passage home,
it is our joy now to grant it.

ARETE:

                              Now, here, sir,
before you go, you must accept our gifts,
so that you will have some small things
to remind you of the Phaecians.

[ARETE *hands* ODYSSEUS *a small box of precious treasure.*]

ODYSSEUS:

                        Great Queen, I thank you,
and farewell; be blest through all your days till age
comes on you. Live in felicity.

ALCINOUS:
Come, Captain, your ship is waiting.

[ODYSSEUS *heads toward the Phaecian ship.* NAUSICAA *catches up with him.*]

NAUSICAA:
Farewell, Odysseus. In your land remember me
who met and saved you. It is worth your thought.

ODYSSEUS:
Daughter of great Alcinous, Nausicaa,
may Zeus grant me daybreak again in my own country!
But there and all my days until I die
may I invoke you as I would a goddess,
Princess, to whom I owe my life.

[*Music. The* PHAECIAN SAILORS *depart with* ODYSSEUS. ALCINOUS, ARETE, *and* NAUSICAA *watch from the shore.*]

ATHENA:
The ship pulled out; the sailors caught the sea as one man.
Hour after hour they flew across the water. But now
slumber, soft and deep, weighed on the wanderer's eyes.
When dawn came, the ship made landfall on Ithaca,
with Odysseus fast asleep.

[ATHENA *exits. Music. The* PHAECIAN SAILORS *carry* ODYSSEUS *off the ship, set his gifts beside him, kneel before him, then reboard their ship, and begin to row.* POSEIDON *enters and addresses* ZEUS.]

POSEIDON:
Father of the Gods, will the bright immortals ever
pay me respect again, if mortals do not?
                                        I warned
the Phaecians long ago not to take passengers
on their black ships across the sea. But now
they have shipped Odysseus homeward
and put him on Ithaca, asleep, with gifts of gold and bronze!

ZEUS:
Little brother, why do you grumble so?
The immortal gods show you no less esteem for this.
If some mortal captain, overcome by pride
of strength cuts or defies you, are you not always free
to take reprisal? Act as your wrath requires and as you will.

POSEIDON:
Then I will wreck this ship within their sight!
Turn her into stone—an island shaped like a ship
off the coast of those Phaecians. Let them gape
at that for generations!

ZEUS:
                    Little brother—

NAUSICAA:
Papa, I see our ship!

103

[*Drums.* POSEIDON *strikes his trident on the ground three times. The* PHAECIAN SAILORS *and their ship turn to stone.* ALCINOUS *and his family watch from the shore.*]

ALCINOUS:
This present doom upon the ship—on me—
my father prophesied in the olden time.
                                        My friends,
we must give up our custom of taking in our ships
poor castaways who land on Scheria; and pray
to Lord Poseidon to leave us passage to the sea.

[*All exit, except the sleeping* ODYSSEUS. ATHENA *enters and stands over him. She makes a gesture to disguise the landscape by enchantment.*]

ATHENA:
When he awoke the landscape looked strange,
unearthly strange, to the lord Odysseus.

[*She exits.*]

ARRIVAL ON ITHACA

ODYSSEUS [*waking*]:
Oh no! My lords and captains of Phaecia
were not those decent men they seemed! By god,
they swore they'd take me home to Ithaca
and did not! What is this outlandish place?
Have they robbed me of my gifts as well?

[*He checks for his treasure.* ATHENA *reenters, disguised as a shepherd boy.* ODYSSEUS *catches sight of her.*]

My child, advise me. Where am I? What is this land?

ATHENA:

                                      Stranger,
you must come from the other end of nowhere,
else you are a great idiot, having to ask
what place this is.

ODYSSEUS:
               Please, child—

ATHENA:
No one would use this ground for training horses,
it is too broken, has no breadth of meadow;
but there is nothing poor about the soil.

ODYSSEUS:
If you could just—

ATHENA:
The yield of grain is wondrous, and wine, too,
with drenching rains and dewfall.

ODYSSEUS:
Please, tell me where—

ATHENA:
                  There's good pasture
for oxen, and water all year long in the cattle ponds.

[ODYSSEUS *starts to leave.*]

For these blessings, friend, Ithaca is well known.

ODYSSEUS [*pausing, then turning*]:
                                        Ithaca?
I've heard of the place, far away in Crete
where I was born. Here is my fortune
with me. I left my sons an equal part
when I shipped out. You see, I killed
Orsilochos, the courier, son of Ido—

ATHENA:
You! You chameleon! You bottomless bag
of tricks! Here in your own country
you cannot give up your dissembling for one instant?

ODYSSEUS:
In Crete, I, I—

ATHENA:
No more of this.

[*She reveals herself.*]

                Haven't you guessed
that I am Pallas Athena, daughter of Zeus?
I, that am always with you in times of trial?

ODYSSEUS:
Once you were fond of me, I'm sure of that,
years ago in Troy. But after that, I never

saw you at my side. You made that speech
to mock me. Am I in truth on Ithaca?

ATHENA [*gesturing to dispel the enchantment of the landscape*]:
Here, I shall make you see the shape of Ithaca:
here is the sea cove of Lord Phorkys,
there is the olive spreading out her leaves
over the inner bay—and there
Mount Neion, with his forest on his back.

[ODYSSEUS *is overcome. He kneels and kisses the ground.*]

ODYSSEUS:
I had not thought to see you ever again.

ATHENA [*urgently*]:
Odysseus, not everything here is right.
There is a crowd of brazen men playing master
in your house, courting your lovely wife.

ODYSSEUS:
And she?

ATHENA:
      Forever grieving for you;
she has allowed her suitors hope,
but her true thoughts are fixed on you.

ODYSSEUS:
I might have bled to death in my own hall,
like Agamemnon, had you not told me this.
Stay by my side.

ATHENA:
                    I shall never leave it;
you'll go forward under my arm when
the moment comes, and I foresee your vast floor
stained with blood.
                    Now, for a while,
I shall transform you;

[*Throughout the following,* ATHENA *removes* ODYSSEUS's *fine Phae-cian cloak and replaces it with a ratty one that* ZEUS *throws down from above. She gives him her shepherd's crook and a pair of spectacles.*]

                    not a soul will know you,
this clear skin of your arms and legs all shriveled,
your chestnut hair all gone, your body dressed
in rags, and the two eyes, that were so brilliant,
dirtied—contemptible you shall seem to everyone.

[*She takes his box of treasure.*]

For now we'll hide your treasure.
Seek out your old swineherd first—
stay with him and question him.

ODYSSEUS [*now stooped and old*]:
But—

ATHENA:
Farewell, Son of Laertes.

EUMAEUS AND NIGHT JOURNEY

[ATHENA *exits. Dogs bark loudly.* EUMAEUS *enters and throws a stone off behind him. The dogs whimper.* EUMAEUS *looks at* ODYSSEUS.]

EUMAEUS:
You might have got torn up there, man!
Two shakes more and a pretty mess for me—
as though I had not trouble enough already
given me by the gods.

ODYSSEUS:
What trouble have the gods given you?

EUMAEUS:
Taken my master, true king that he was.
I hang on here, still mourning for him, raising pigs
of his to feed strangers.
                              Come to the cabin.
You must eat something, drink some wine, and tell me
where you are from and the hard times you've seen.

ODYSSEUS:
May Zeus and all the gods give you your heart's desire
for taking me in so kindly, friend.

[*During the following,* EUMAEUS *brings out chairs and food for his guest.* ATHENA, *invisible, reenters and comes in to lie on the floor and listen. She loves* EUMAEUS. *As* EUMAEUS *and* ODYSSEUS *speak, evening falls, and it grows dark.*]

EUMAEUS:

                                   Tush, friend,
all wanderers and beggars come from Zeus.
What we can give is slight but well meant—
all we dare.
                 I told you
the gods, long ago, hindered our lord's return.
He had a fondness for me, would have pensioned me
with acres of my own, a house, a wife that other men
admired and courted.
                          But the man's gone.
He took ship overseas for the wild horse country
of Troy to fight the Trojans.

ODYSSEUS:

                              Tell me,
who is this lord, so rich and powerful
as you describe him? Perhaps I've seen him:
I have roamed about the world for so long.

EUMAEUS:

                                      Well, man,
neither his lady nor his son nor I will put stock
in any news of him brought back by a beggar.
Wandering men tell lies for a night's lodging,
for fresh clothing; truth doesn't interest them.
Every time some traveler comes ashore
he has to tell my mistress his pretty tale.
No: long ago wild dogs and carrion birds,
most like, laid bare his ribs on land;
or it may be quick fishes picked him clean

[*He looks directly at* ODYSSEUS.]

in the deep sea—Odysseus, I mean.
For all he was a warrior, his heart was mild.
That is how he was.

ODYSSEUS:

                Friend,
let me not merely talk as others talk
but swear to it: your lord is now at hand
and he will be avenged on any who dishonor
his wife and son. I swear—

EUMAEUS:

                    Ah, he's another
to be distressed about—Odysseus's son,
Telemachus.

ODYSSEUS:
Oh?

EUMAEUS:
Someone, god òr man, upset him, made him
rash, so that he sailed away to Sparta
to hear news of his father.

ODYSSEUS:
He sailed away? For news of his father?

EUMAEUS:
Yes.

ODYSSEUS:
All the way to Sparta?

EUMAEUS:
Yes, poor boy.

ODYSSEUS:
But still, that's very brave.

EUMAEUS:
Come, let us talk now of other things. No more
imaginings. It makes me heavyhearted.
Tell me, now: Who are you and how did you
come to Ithaca? I don't suppose
you walked here on the sea.

ATHENA:
To this, the master of improvisation
answered you, O my swineherd,
how he was born illegitimately—

ODYSSEUS:
in Crete.

ATHENA:
How he

ODYSSEUS:
accidentally killed a man

ATHENA:
before he was

ODYSSEUS:
kidnapped by pirates

ATHENA:
and brought to

ODYSSEUS:
Thesprotia.

ATHENA:
Where

ODYSSEUS:
in the king's house I heard news of Odysseus,
who was lately a guest there, passing by
on his way home, the king said.

ATHENA:
And Odysseus went on, as evening fell,
to describe how

ODYSSEUS:
the Thesprotians robbed

ATHENA:
him as he was going home, and threw him

ODYSSEUS:
overboard

ATHENA:
and how he

ATHENA AND ODYSSEUS:
swam to Ithaca.

EUMAEUS:
                    Ah well, poor drifter,
you've made me sad with your hard life
and all your wanderings. That bit about Odysseus
being alive, though, you might have spared me;
you won't make me believe that. Thesprotians, yes,
but—

ODYSSEUS:
A black suspicious heart beats in you surely.
Promise me, if you ever find I lied to you,
you'll pitch me down from some high rock
to teach the next poor man not to lie.

EUMAEUS:
                                    Friend,
if I agreed to that, a great name
I should acquire in the world for goodness.
How confidently, after that, should I
kneel down to pray.
                    Come, lie down and rest,
have my cloak—
we're in for bad weather tonight, lie down.
I think I should stay out with the swine.

[EUMAEUS *exits.* ODYSSEUS *lies down to sleep. Music.*]

ATHENA:
Now night came on: rough with no moon.

Honeyed sleep took Odysseus in her arms.
But Athena, ever sleepless, flew to his son to
guide him home from Menelaus.

[TELEMACHUS *enters, saying farewell to* MENELAUS. *Various* SUITORS *enter and position themselves like islands scattered in the sea. They are on the lookout for* TELEMACHUS. ATHENA *leads* TELEMACHUS *away from* MENELAUS *and safely around each of the* SUITORS *to Ithaca as she speaks.*]

Thus they sailed from Sparta, past
Krouni and Khalkis with its lovely streams.
With Athena disguised as Mentor at the helm
they picked their way through darkness,
and she guided them far from the treacherous straits
where the suitors lay with ambush and murder in their hearts.
When dawn arose, they found themselves near Ithaca.

[TELEMACHUS *exits with* ATHENA. *The* SUITORS *exit, very frustrated. Music ends.*]

REUNION

[*It is morning.* EUMAEUS *enters.* ODYSSEUS *is lying awake.*]

EUMAEUS:
Good morning, friend.

ODYSSEUS:
Good morning, Eumaeus.

Eumaeus, I would be
grateful if you'd show me the way to town.
If I go as far as the great hall of King Odysseus
I might tell Queen Penelope my news.
Or I can drift inside among the suitors
to see what alms they give, rich as they are—

EUMAEUS:

Friend, friend,
how could this fantasy take hold of you?
You're playing with your life and nothing less
if you feel drawn to mingle in that company—
reckless, violent, and famous for it
out to the rim of heaven.

ODYSSEUS:
May you be dear to Zeus for this, Eumaeus,
even as you are to me.
But come now,
tell me: What of your lord Odysseus's father?
After twenty years, is he still alive?

EUMAEUS:
Old Laertes lives out in the country,
away from town. Alone and heartbroken
for a son long gone, and for his wife. Sorrow
enfeebled him when she died.

[TELEMACHUS *enters upstage with a* SAILOR *and addresses him.*]

TELEMACHUS:
Take the ship around the point to town,

but leave me here to walk inland
as Lord Mentor advised. Later this evening,
after looking at my farms,
I'll join you in the city. Farewell.

[*The* SAILOR *exits.* TELEMACHUS *approaches* EUMAEUS*'s hut.*]

ODYSSEUS:
                                            Eumaeus,
I hear footsteps—some friend, for the dogs
are snuffling belly down; not one has even growled.

EUMAEUS [*seeing* TELEMACHUS *and leaving the hut*]:
Light of my days, Telemachus,
you made it back! Come in, dear child,
and let me feast my eyes!
How rarely you come to visit me
and your woods and pastures!

TELEMACHUS:
I am with you now, Eumaeus. See,
I have come because I wanted to see you first,
to hear from you if Mother stayed at home—
or is she married and Odysseus's bed left empty
for some gloomy spider's weaving?

EUMAEUS:
Telemachus, you know your mother is not married.
She will never marry again. Now come inside.

[ODYSSEUS *begins to rise, to offer his seat to* TELEMACHUS.]

TELEMACHUS:

Keep your seat, friend, I'm sure I can sit
on the ground.

        So Eumaeus,
what's your friend's home port? How did he come?
I doubt he came walking on the sea.

EUMAEUS:

His home is Crete, but he has knocked about the world.
Just now he broke away from a shipload
of Thesprotians to reach my hut. I place him
in your hands. He desires your protection.

TELEMACHUS:

                       Eumaeus, my protection?
The idea cuts me to the heart. It's impossible
to let him stay among the suitors. They might
injure him—and how could I bear that?

ODYSSEUS:

                   Kind prince,
it may be fitting for me to speak a word. These fellows
riding roughshod over you in your own house,
admirable as you are, how is it possible?
Are you resigned to being bled? Are the townsmen
stirred up against you? What of your brothers?

TELEMACHUS:

No, no, there is no rancor in the town against me,
but the suitors are too many, too powerful
and united in their cause. As to brothers—

single sons are the rule in our family;
Laertes had but one, and he had me.
                                        Eumaeus,
can you go down at once and tell the Lady Penelope
that I am back? But don't let any of the suitors
hear it; they have a mind to do me harm.

EUMAEUS:
Should I not call on your grandfather Laertes
and tell him the news?

TELEMACHUS:
                        Have Mother send
Eurycleia on the quiet out to tell him.

ODYSSEUS [*astonished*]:
Eurycleia?

TELEMACHUS:
My father's nurse—mine as well.

ODYSSEUS:
She's still alive?

TELEMACHUS:
Oh, yes. [*To* EUMAEUS] Then hurry back.

EUMAEUS:
I'll be back before nightfall.

[EUMAEUS *exits.* ATHENA *enters and signals* ODYSSEUS *to join her outside the hut.*]

ODYSSEUS:
Excuse me, Prince Telemachus, I have
something I forgot to tell our friend.

TELEMACHUS:
Please, go on.

[ODYSSEUS *leaves the hut.* TELEMACHUS *lies down to rest.*]

ATHENA:
Odysseus, the time has come. Dissemble
to your son no longer. Tell him how you two together
will bring doom on the suitors in the town.
I will make you lithe and young, restore
your bright eyes and your hair.

[ATHENA *removes* ODYSSEUS's *old cloak and gives him the new one.
She removes his spectacles. He is rejuvenated.*]

Now go! I'm eager for the fight!

[ATHENA *sits with her back to the scene.* ODYSSEUS *enters the hut.*
TELEMACHUS *wakes and is very frightened. He cowers.*]

TELEMACHUS:
                    Stranger,
you are no longer what you were just now!
Your cloak is new, even your skin! You are
one of the gods who rule the sweep of heaven!
Have mercy on us!

ODYSSEUS:
No god. Why take me for a god? No, no.
Telemachus, it is only I, your old father,
I am Odysseus, come back.

TELEMACHUS:
                              Odysseus?
You? You cannot be my father! Meddling
spirits have conceived this trick to twist
the knife in me! No man of woman born
could work these wonders. I swear,
you were in rags and old—

ODYSSEUS:
This is not like a prince—to be swept away
in wonder in his father's presence.

TELEMACHUS:
Go away!

ODYSSEUS [*approaching slowly*]:
No other Odysseus will ever come,
for he and I are one, the same; his bitter
fortune and his wanderings are mine—

TELEMACHUS:
No, no!

ODYSSEUS [*catching his son in his arms*]:
Believe me, dear Telemachus:
I am that which you lacked in childhood
and suffered pain for lack of.

I am your father.
Twenty years are gone and I am back home
on my own island.
As for my change of skin,
that is a charm Athena uses as she will;
she has the knack of making me a beggar man
sometimes, and sometimes young,
with finer clothes about me.
It's no hard thing for the gods of heaven
to glorify a man or bring him low.

[ATHENA *turns where she is sitting.*]

ATHENA:

Now from
the well of longing in both men cries came up,
like those made by a great taloned hawk
when a farmer comes to take her nestlings from her
before they can fly away. So helplessly they cried
and would have gone on till sundown
had not Telemachus said,

TELEMACHUS:

Dear Father, tell me
what kind of vessel put you here ashore on Ithaca?
I doubt you made it walking on the sea.

ODYSSEUS:
Only plain truth shall I tell you, child.

[ATHENA *signals* ODYSSEUS *to hurry along.*]

But we'll have to wait. The goddess Athena herself
has directed me to plot with you how we
should kill the suitors.

TELEMACHUS:
                 Father, all my life your fame
as a fighting man has echoed in my ears,
but what you speak of is a staggering thing,
beyond imagining. How can the two of us defeat
a house full of men in their prime?

ODYSSEUS:
It's true, we only have two allies, but their
names are Zeus and Athena.
Here's your part: at daybreak, go on home,
go mingle with our princes.
The swineherd later will bring me there—
a beggar by my looks. If they make fun of me
or injure me, do nothing;
let your ribs cage up your springing heart,
no matter what I suffer. Then, at night,
round up all our old weapons and armor—
leave them no arms in the great hall.
                      Now one more thing.
If you are my son and blood, let no one hear
I am about. Not my father Laertes, nor the
swineherd here, nor Penelope herself.

[ODYSSEUS *and* TELEMACHUS *exit.*]

ATHENA:
So their talk ran on, while back at the hall,
the suitors had now returned.

[ATHENA *runs off.*]

ANTINOUS ENRAGED

[*Drums. The palace of* ODYSSEUS. *The* SUITORS *enter, led by* AN-
TINOUS, *enraged.*]

ANTINOUS:
Damn him! How did we miss him?
All day long we had lookouts posted,
and every hour a fresh pair of eyes;
at night we never slept ashore but after sundown
cruised the open water patrolling until dawn!
Meanwhile, some spirit brings him home!

[PENELOPE *enters, unnoticed.*]

Well, let this company plan his destruction,
and leave him no way out—

PENELOPE:
              Madman!
How dare you plot against my son
in his own house? Have you no piety? In Ithaca
they say you are the best of your generation
in mind and speech. Not so, you never were.

How can you forget that your own father
fled to us when the realm was up in arms
against him? Only Odysseus took him in.
Yet it is Odysseus's house you now consume,
his son you kill, or try to kill. And me
you ravage now, and grieve. I call upon you
to make an end of it!

ANTINOUS:

                    Penelope, wise daughter
of Icarios, dismiss these terrors from your mind.
I say that man does not exist, nor will, who
dares lay hands upon your son while I live,
walk the earth, and use my eyes.
For it is true: when I was young, Odysseus
took me on his knees and fed me often—
tidbits and red wine.

                    Tell the boy
he must not tremble for his life,
at least not so long as he is alone in the
suitors' company. If heaven wills his death
by other means, well, nothing can be done.

PENELOPE:
Antinous, it's growing dark. Get out.

ANTINOUS:
Until tomorrow, then, wise Penelope.
Sweet dreams.

[*The* SUITORS *leave.* TELEMACHUS *enters unseen.*]

TELEMACHUS [*whispering*]:
Mother—

PENELOPE:
       Back with me!
Telemachus, more sweet to me than sunlight!
I thought I should not see you ever again,
after you left without a word!

TELEMACHUS:
Mother, not now. My heart already aches—

PENELOPE:
What happened? What happened?

TELEMACHUS:
I went to the palace of Menelaus—
Mother, you should see it—but he
takes no pleasure in his wealth.
And I saw Helen there, Helen of Troy.

PENELOPE:
But Odysseus? Is he alive?

TELEMACHUS:
           I'll tell you everything
I heard, as Menelaus says he heard it
from the Ancient of the Sea.

[*They exit.*]

ARGOS

[*Music. The next morning, outside the walls of* ODYSSEUS'*s palace.*
Enter ODYSSEUS *and* EUMAEUS. ARGOS *the dog lies on the ground at a*
little distance.]

EUMAEUS:
My friend, here is Odysseus's hall. I've brought
you here as my prince commanded—the gods alone
know why. But I must ask you one more time:
Wouldn't you rather go back into the country
and let me make a farmhand of you?

ODYSSEUS:
Thank you, Eumaeus. But I am curious
to see the place. Please lead the way.

[*Two* SUITORS *enter from inside the palace.*]

FIRST SUITOR:
Look at that! One scurvy type leading another.
The gods pair them off every time. Hey swineherd!
Where are you taking your new pig?

SECOND SUITOR:
How many doorposts has he rubbed
his back on, whining for garbage?

EUMAEUS:
What courtly ways you have! What manners!
Let our true lord come back, he'll teach you
how to speak!

SECOND SUITOR:
>   Look how the dog can snap!
> Odysseus is dead. He died at sea.

ODYSSEUS:
> Calm yourself, Eumaeus, I am used to it.
> Lead the way.

[*The* SUITORS *exit, laughing.* EUMAEUS *and* ODYSSEUS *make to enter the palace but stop when* ODYSSEUS *notices* ARGOS.]

ATHENA:
>   As he spoke
> an old dog, lying near, pricked up his ears
> and lifted up his muzzle. This was Argos,
> trained as a puppy by Odysseus,
> but never taken on a hunt before
> his master sailed for Troy.
> Treated as rubbish now, old Argos lay
> in the filth before the gates, abandoned
> and half destroyed by flies.
>   But when he heard
> Odysseus's voice nearby, he did his best
> to wag his tail, nose down, with flattened ears,
> though he lacked the strength
> to move toward him whom even the gods
> could not disguise enough.

[ODYSSEUS *recognizes his dog. He goes to him.*]

ODYSSEUS:

                Eumaeus,
it is very bad to see a dog like this.
He would have been a fine dog, from the look of him,
though I can't say as to his power and speed
when he was young. He has a hunter's build,
not like a table dog landowners keep for style.

EUMAEUS:

If this old hound could show the form he had
when Lord Odysseus left him, heading for Troy,
you'd see him swift and strong.
He never shrank from any savage thing
he brought to bay in the deep woods. Now misery
has him in leash. His master died abroad,
and no one here to have a care for him.
He seems to like you well enough.

[HERMES *enters as* EUMAEUS *leaves.*]

ATHENA:

                With this,
Eumaeus left him and entered the great house.
But death and darkness in that instant closed
the eyes of Argos, who had seen his master,
Odysseus, after twenty years.

[HERMES *lifts* ARGOS *and carries him off.*]

BEGGAR AT THE PALACE

[ODYSSEUS *enters the palace.* ATHENA *follows, unseen. Music. The* SUITORS *are lolling about, in their dirty way.* TELEMACHUS *sits in a corner.* EUMAEUS *approaches.* ODYSSEUS *lags behind.*]

EUMAEUS:
Telemachus, our guest is in the palace.

TELEMACHUS [*handing* EUMAEUS *some bread and a wooden bowl*]:
Give this to him. But tell him
to go among the suitors on his own;
shyness is no asset to a hungry man.

EUMAEUS [*handing the things to* ODYSSEUS]:
                                        Friend,
Telemachus is pleased to give you this,
but he commands you to approach the suitors
and try—

[*The* SUITORS *catch sight of* ODYSSEUS *and* EUMAEUS.]

ANTINOUS:
            Oh look, the breeder of pigs!
Eumaeus, why have you brought your swine inside?
Are we not plagued enough with beggars,
foragers, and rats? You find the company
too slow at eating up your lord's estate—
so you bring this scarecrow in?

[*The* SUITORS *laugh.*]

EUMAEUS:
                              Antinous,
you are well born, but that was not well said.
You are a hard man, and you always were,
more so than others of this company—hard
on all Odysseus's people and on me. But—

TELEMACHUS:
Be still, Eumaeus, don't answer this man.
Antinous, I appreciate your fatherly concern
on my behalf, and your anxiety
that I should order a poor stranger from my house.
God forbid such a thing!
No, I call on you to give. And spare your qualms
as to my mother's loss, and mine—
but there's no such idea in your head.

ANTINOUS:
Telemachus, you let your tongue and temper
run away with you. If every man
gave as much as I should like to, this man would
be kept for months—kept out of sight!

[*The* SUITORS *laugh.* ATHENA *enters, invisible.*]

ODYSSEUS [*approaching* ANTINOUS]:
Spare me a little, sir. I take you for
the richest here, you look like a king.
Let me speak well of you as I pass on
over the boundless earth. I, too, had
fortune once, lived well, stood well
with men, and gave alms often

to poor wanderers like the one you see before you.
But Zeus the son of Chronos brought me down—

ANTINOUS:
God! What evil wind blew in this pest!
Nudge at my table, will you, you nosing rat?

[*He knocks the alms bowl from* ODYSSEUS*'s hand.*]

SUITOR ONE [*alarmed*]:
Antinous—

ODYSSEUS:
It is a pity, sir, that you have no heart.
You sit here, fat on another man's meat,
and cannot bring yourself to rummage out
a crust of bread for me. I was wrong to—

[*He starts to go.*]

ANTINOUS:
                                        Now!
You think you'll shuffle off and get away
after that, you bundle of rags and lice?
Oh no you don't!

[ANTINOUS *picks up a stool and throws it at* ODYSSEUS, *but* ATHENA
knocks it aside at the last moment. EUMAEUS *runs off.*]

SUITOR ONE:
Antinous, you were wrong to strike
this famished tramp. What if he happened

to be a god? You know they go in foreign guise,
looking like strangers—

SUITOR TWO [*interceding*]:
Here we are, almost at blows about a beggar man,
and our pleasure in an evening's entertainment
about to be spoiled—

[*Everyone settles down,* TELEMACHUS *and* ODYSSEUS *in separate
parts of the room.* EUMAEUS *and* PENELOPE *enter above and look
down at the hall.*]

EUMAEUS [*to* PENELOPE]:
               There, my queen,
there is the unfortunate tramp come wandering
through the house. The suitors are mistreating him,
Antinous most of all.

PENELOPE:
Go to him on my behalf, Eumaeus,
tell him I wish to greet and question him.
Abroad in the great world, he may have heard
rumors about Odysseus—

EUMAEUS:
               Indeed,
he claims he has, but I say—

[TELEMACHUS *sneezes loudly.*]

PENELOPE:
Did you hear that, Eumaeus? My son
has sneezed a blessing on what I said.
Go call the stranger straight to me.

[PENELOPE *and* EUMAEUS *exit.*]

TELEMACHUS:
Come now, gentlemen. You've dined well.
It's growing dark and time for you to go on home.
Soon enough, tomorrow, you can begin again.

[*The* SUITORS *trail out.*]

INTERVIEW

[EUMAEUS *reenters. The* MAIDS *are straightening up the hall.*]

EUMAEUS [*to* ODYSSEUS]:
Friend, our queen would like to hear your tale,
if you will wait in the hall. She'll shelter you tonight.

[*To* TELEMACHUS] Dear Prince, I must go home to look to my affairs.
Both of you, consider your own safety first,
take care not to get hurt.

[EURYCLEIA *enters.*]

TELEMACHUS:
                    Your wish is mine, Eumaeus.

[EUMAEUS *exits.*]

Nurse, go shut the women in their quarters
while I shift Father's armor back
to the inner rooms. I want them shielded
from the draft and smoke.

EURYCLEIA:
      It is time, child,
you took an interest in such things.

[*To* ODYSSEUS, *kindly*] Good evening, sir.

[*To the* MAIDS] Go on, now, go on!

[EURYCLEIA *and the* MAIDS *exit.* ATHENA *enters and holds still, one arm raised above her head holding a lantern.*]

TELEMACHUS:
      Oh, Father,
one of the gods of heaven is in this place.
The walls and roof beams are all glowing,
as though lit by a fire blazing near.

ODYSSEUS:
Be still: keep still about it—but remember it.
Now clear the hall of all our old arms—
then off to bed. Your mother will be down soon.

TELEMACHUS:
Until tomorrow, then.

[TELEMACHUS *exits with some of the arms.* MELANTHO, *one of the* MAIDS, *enters.* ATHENA *withdraws.*]

MELANTHO:

Ah, stranger,
are you still here, so creepy, hanging around
late at night, looking the women over?
You old goat, go outside—get out of here!

ODYSSEUS:

Little devil,
why set on me like this? Because I go
unwashed and wear these rags,
and make the rounds? But so I must—

MELANTHO:
Go on, I'll set the dogs on you!

PENELOPE [*entering*]:

Oh, shameless,
through and through! And do you think me blind,
blind to your conduct? You knew I waited—
you heard me say it—waited to see this man
and question him about my lord.
Go on with you!

[MELANTHO *exits.* PENELOPE *calls off.*]

Alcippe! Please bring a rug here for our guest.
I wish to have his whole story.

[*To* ODYSSEUS] Sir, do you tell fortunes?

ODYSSEUS:
I'm afraid, kind lady, that I do not have that art.

PENELOPE:
Do you tell lies?

ODYSSEUS:
If I have, in my life, sometimes made up stories,
I would not do so now to you.

[ALCIPPE, *a* MAID, *enters with a small rug and unrolls it.* ODYSSEUS
and PENELOPE *sit.* ATHENA *sits, unseen, in the shadows.* ALCIPPE *exits.*]

PENELOPE:
Will I offend you if I make so bold as to ask you
directly who you are and where you come from?
Of what country and what parents were you born?

ODYSSEUS:
My lady, never a man in the wide world
should have a fault to find with you. Your name
has gone out under heaven like the sweet
honor of some god-fearing king, who rules
so wisely that his black lands bear
both wheat and barley, the trees are heavy
with bright fruit, and the deep sea
gives up great hauls of fish by his good strategy,
so all his folk fare well.

This being so,
let it suffice to ask me of other matters—
not my blood, my homeland.
My heart is sore; but I must not be found
sitting in tears here, in another's house.

PENELOPE:

Stranger, as to your praise of me,
my looks, my face, my carriage, were destroyed
when my husband crossed the sea to Troy.
If he returned, if he were here to care for me—
I might be what you claim!
But heaven sent me grief instead. These suitors
that you see around the hall consume this house,
all the while pressing me to marry.

ODYSSEUS:
But how have you kept them off?

PENELOPE:

At first, tricks served my turn
to draw the time out. I had the happy thought
to set up weaving a close-grained web
on my big loom in the hall. I said, that day:
"Young men—my suitors—now my lord is dead,
let me finish my weaving before I marry,
or else my thread will have been spun in vain.
It is a shroud I weave for Lord Laertes—Odysseus's father—
for when cold Death comes to lay his hand on him.
The country wives would hold me in dishonor

if he, with all his fortune, lay unshrouded."
I reached their hearts that way, and they agreed.
So every day I wove on the great loom,
but every night by torchlight I unwove it;
and so for three years I deceived the Acheans.
But when the seasons brought a fourth year on,
one of my slinking maids caught on to me.
I had no choice then but to finish it.
And now, as matters stand at last,
I have no strength left to evade a marriage, I
can't find any further way; my parents
urge it upon me, and my son
cannot stand by while they eat up his property.

But now, I insist,

confide in me. Tell me your ancestry.
You weren't born out of an oak or a stone.

ODYSSEUS:
Honorable lady, will you not be satisfied
until I give you my pedigree?

PENELOPE:
No.

ODYSSEUS:
    Well then, I will tell you.
One of the great islands of the world
in midsea, in the wine-dark sea, is Crete—

ATHENA:

As the night wore on, the stranger spoke
of far-off lands, of the storms that brought
him low, and finally of—

ODYSSEUS:

                        Odysseus.
I saw him with my own eyes once at Knossos.
Gales had caught him off Cape Malea—

ATHENA:

Now all these lies he made appear so truthful
that, as she listened, Penelope began to weep. The skin
of her pale face grew moist the way pure snow
softens and glistens on the mountains, thawed
by the south wind after powdering from the west,
and, as the snow melts, mountain streams run full:
so her white cheeks were wetted by these tears
shed for her lord Odysseus—sitting by her side.

PENELOPE:

                     I think that I shall say, friend,
give me some proof. If you saw my lord, tell me
how he looked, give me some particular.

ODYSSEUS:

Lady, so long a time has passed—

PENELOPE:

Give me some particular.

ODYSSEUS:

He wore a brooch
with a work of art on its face: a hunting dog
pinning a spotted fawn between his forepaws—
wonderful to see how it seemed the deer convulsed,
with wild hooves flying, though she was made of gold,
and nothing more.

PENELOPE:

With my own hands
I pinned that brooch on him. Now, I suppose,
it lies beneath the sea.

ODYSSEUS:

Dear lady, that may be, it may.
But know that if it does, he still holds its image
in his mind. It is not lost.

PENELOPE:

My lord is dead.

ODYSSEUS:
Listen. Weep no more and listen:
I have a thing to tell you, something true.
I heard but lately of your lord's return,
heard that he is alive, among Thesprotians
in their green land amassing fortune
to bring home. His company went down
in a shipwreck, but he was spared. You see,
he is alive and well, and headed homeward now.
Indeed he is very close.

PENELOPE:

              Ah, stranger,
if what you say could ever happen!
But my heart tells me what must be.
Odysseus will not come to me; no ship
will be prepared for you. We have no master
quick to receive and furnish out a guest
as Lord Odysseus was.

              Or did I dream him?
Come, friend, we will prepare a bath for you—

ODYSSEUS:

No, no. I have no longing for a footbath.
I would not like any of your young maids
to touch me. But if there is an old one, old and wise,
who has lived through suffering as I have,
I would not mind being touched by her.

PENELOPE:

There is such a one.

             [*Calling off*] Eurycleia!
Please prepare a footbath for our friend.

[*She gazes at* ODYSSEUS.]

Dear guest, no foreign man so sympathetic
ever came to my house, no guest more likable,
so wry and humble are the things you say.

[EURYCLEIA *and* ALCIPPE *enter with a chair, a pitcher of water, and a
bowl.* ALCIPPE *sets down her things and leaves.*]

Here is an old maidservant who nursed my lord.
She took him into her arms the hour he was born.

[PENELOPE *moves aside.*]

EURYCLEIA:
The queen Penelope, Icarios's daughter, bids me:
so let me bathe your feet to serve my lady—
to serve you too.

[EURYCLEIA *begins to bathe* ODYSSEUS's *feet.*]

          I must tell you
my heart within me stirs. Strangers have come here,
many through the years, but no one ever came, I swear,
who seemed so like Odysseus—body, voice, and limbs—
as you do.

ODYSSEUS:
        That is what they say.
All who have seen the two of us remark
how like we are, as you yourself have said—

[ATHENA *sees that* EURYCLEIA *is about to uncover* ODYSSEUS's *scar.*
She runs forward, covers PENELOPE's *eyes, and turns her face away.*
Only ODYSSEUS *sees and hears her.*]

ATHENA:
Odysseus, watch out! The scar! Your scar!

EURYCLEIA [*seeing the scar*]:
What's this?

ODYSSEUS:
Nurse—

EURYCLEIA:
Odysseus—it's you! Oh, yes! It's y—

[ODYSSEUS *leaps up and holds* EURYCLEIA *around the throat.* PENELOPE *sees none of it.*]

ODYSSEUS:
                            Will you destroy me,
Nurse, who gave me milk at your own breast?
You found me out—keep it from the others,
else I warn you, and I mean it too,
I'll kill you, nurse or not, I'll kill you!

EURYCLEIA [*breaking free and scolding*]:
Child, whom do you think you're talking to?
Who do you think I am—to speak to me like this?
I'll be as silent as a stone. Now you sit down!
Be quiet. Before she notices.

[ODYSSEUS *sits.* ATHENA *uncovers* PENELOPE'S *eyes.*]

PENELOPE:
                          Friend, I know the time
for sleep is coming soon, but let me ask you this—
you seem so wise:
                    Shall I stay beside my
son and honor my lord's bed? Or had I best
join fortunes with a suitor? Is it time for that?

ODYSSEUS:
Dear lady—

PENELOPE:
No. Here is what I shall do.
                              Tomorrow
I shall decree a contest for the day.
We have twelve ax heads. In his time, my lord
could line them up, all twelve, at intervals,
like a ship's ribbing; then he'd back away
a long way off and whip an arrow through.
Now I'll impose this trial on the suitors.
The one who easily handles and strings the bow
and shoots through all twelve axes I shall marry,
whoever he may be—then look my last
on this my first love's beautiful brimming house.
But I'll remember, though I dream it only.

ODYSSEUS:
This is an excellent plan. Let there be no
postponement of the trial. Odysseus,
who knows the shifts of combat,
will be here long before any of those boys
can stretch or string that bow.

PENELOPE:
                              If you were willing
to sit with me and comfort me, my friend,
no tide of sleep would ever close my eyes.
But mortals cannot go forever sleepless.
Upstairs I go, then, to my single bed,

my sighing bed. You can stretch out
on the bare floor, or else command a bed.

ATHENA:
So she went up to her chamber, softly lit,
accompanied by Eurycleia,
and the house grew quiet.

[PENELOPE *and* EURYCLEIA *exit.* ODYSSEUS *lies down.* ATHENA *goes to stand over him.*]

But Odysseus could not sleep.
He rocked himself, rolling from side to side,
as a cook turns a sausage, casting about
to see how he alone could defeat his enemies.

[*To* ODYSSEUS] Why so wakeful?
Here is your home, there lies your lady,
and your son is here, as fine as one could wish!

ODYSSEUS [*sitting up*]:
Goddess, I am one man, how can I defeat
so many? They are always here in force.
And if I can kill them, where could I go for safety?
Their brothers and fathers will rise up against me!

ATHENA:
What touching faith! Another man would trust
some villainous mortal with no brains more than
you trust me!

146

ODYSSEUS:
Goddess, how can I—

ATHENA:
Sleep, Odysseus!

[ATHENA *waves her hand in anger and impatience, and* ODYSSEUS
faints dead away. She exits.]

THE CONTEST

[*Music. It is dawn. The misbehaving* MAIDS *run into the palace, followed closely by the* SUITORS. ODYSSEUS *wakes and scoots off to a
corner.* EUMAEUS, *the blind singer* PHEMIOS, *and* ATHENA *(invisible)
also enter. The music and dance of the* SUITORS' *first entrance are
reprised but at their climax are interrupted by* TELEMACHUS.]

TELEMACHUS:
Gentlemen! This is not a public house,
but the palace of Odysseus—my inheritance!
Today you will treat my home and my friends well.
If not—

EURYMACHUS:
Of course, we will, Telemachus.
Here, let me give your guests a bath!

[*He throws his drink in the faces of* EUMAEUS *and* ODYSSEUS.]

TELEMACHUS:
Do that again, Eurymachus,
and your father will have a funeral here
instead of a wedding.

You others, I will suffer no
more viciousness against a guest.
I know what is honorable and what is not.
My childhood is over.

ATHENA:
                              At this,
Pallas Athena touched off in the suitors
an uncontrollable fit of laughter.

[*Music. The* SUITORS *begin to laugh, slowly, silently. Their faces are distorted; they fall to the ground.*]

She drove them into a nightmare; they laughed
with jaws that were no longer theirs,
while blood splattered their meat
and blurring tears flooded their eyes.

PHEMIOS:
O lost sad men, what terror is this you suffer?
Night shrouds you to the knees, your heads,
your faces; death runs round you, the entryway
is thick with shades—

[PENELOPE *enters carrying* ODYSSEUS's *old bow. Music ends. The spell is broken. The* SUITORS *laugh out loud, in their usual nasty way.*]

PENELOPE:
                    My lords, hear me:
Suitors indeed, you've commandeered this house
to feast and drink in, day and night. You have
no justification for yourselves—none
except your lust to marry me. Very well, then.
Here I am. Come forward, gentlemen.
I now declare a contest for the prize:
Here is my lord Odysseus's hunting bow.
Whoever can bend and string it, then send
an arrow through the sockets of twelve
iron ax heads, I will marry, and leave this
place forever.
                    Eumaeus,
give my lord's bow to the suitors.

EUMAEUS [*upset*]:
Lord Odysseus's bow?

PENELOPE:
Take it, dear Eumaeus.

[*He can't. The* MAIDS *have set the ax heads.* TELEMACHUS *steps up
and takes the bow, feigning a kind of hysterical despair.*]

TELEMACHUS:
Step up, my lords, contend now for your prize!
There is no woman like her in Achea,
nor in Pylos, nor in Mycenae,
neither in Ithaca nor on all the mainland!
Come on, no hanging back!

ANTINOUS:

Now one man at a time go forward
and try the bow. Leodes?

[*The suitor* LEODES *takes the bow. He tries three times to string it,
but* ATHENA, *invisible, prevents him with a light touch of her finger
on his hand. He gives up.*]

LEODES:

Friends, I cannot. Let the next man handle it.
Here is a bow to break the heart and spirit
of many strong men. Aye, death is less
bitter than to—

ANTINOUS:

          What a preposterous speech!
You can't string the weapon, so you say,
"Here is a bow to break your hearts!"
Crushing thought! You were not born—
you never had it in you—to pull that bow
or let an arrow fly. Who's next?

[*Another* SUITOR *comes forward.* ODYSSEUS *pulls* EUMAEUS *aside.
The* SUITOR *tries the bow.* ATHENA *puts her finger on his hand.*]

ODYSSEUS:

Eumaeus, would you be man enough
to stand by Odysseus if he came back?
Suppose he dropped out of a clear sky, as I did;
suppose some god should bring him home—
would you bear arms for him?

EUMAEUS:

                         Ah, let the master come!
Then judge what stuff is in me, and how I manage arms!

ODYSSEUS:

Do you believe a goddess can change
a man's appearance any way she wills?

EUMAEUS:

I am certain of it.

[*The* SUITOR *gives up, and another* SUITOR *tries the bow. He meets the same fate as the others.*]

ODYSSEUS:

                    Then know, Eumaeus,
Odysseus is home, for I am he. I am ashore
in my own land—helped by Athena and other men.
Look, here is the scar from the tusk wound of
that old boar, the day we hunted on Parnassos—
do you remember?

EUMAEUS:

                    Odysseus? Can it—?

ODYSSEUS:

Hush, now. Go on and drift outside. Bolt the outer
gate, then drift back in—and bolt these doors
behind you. Do you hear?

EUMAEUS:

                    Yes, Odysseus. But how—

[*Another* SUITOR *tries the bow.*]

ODYSSEUS:
No time now, Eumaeus. Hurry! Go on!

SUITOR [*failing at the bow*]:
Curse this day! We cannot even string the bow!
How will we be spoken of in times to come?

ANTINOUS:
Come to yourself. You know, this is a holy day,
no day to sweat over a bowstring.
                                          Keep your head.
Postpone the bow. Let us celebrate now, keep the bow
safe overnight and try again tomorrow—

[ANTINOUS *takes the bow, and the* SUITORS *prepare to leave with it.*]

ODYSSEUS:
My lords, contenders for the queen, permit me:
let me test my fingers and my pull
to see if I have any strength left at all,
or if my roving life has robbed me of it.

ANTINOUS:
You bleary drunken vagabond, are you insane?
Aren't you coddled here enough, at table
taking meat with gentlemen, your betters,
and listening to our talk as no other tramp has done?
Don't touch that bow, I warn you—

PENELOPE:

Antinous, discourtesy is never handsome.
What are you afraid of?
Suppose this exile put his back into it
and managed to string the bow.
Could he then take me home to be his bride?
He can't imagine that, so how can you? Don't
let the thought spoil your dinner, Antinous,
give the man a try.

ANTINOUS:

                Penelope, daughter of Icarios,
we are not given to fantasy. But think of it,
a beggar, out of nowhere, competing with us?
What of our reputations?

PENELOPE:

You have no reputation left in this realm,
Antinous, nor the faintest hope of ever gaining
it again. Why hang your heads over this,
after abusing another man's house for years?
This stranger is a big man, well compacted,
and claims to be of noble blood.
Ai! Give him the bow, let's have it out!

TELEMACHUS:

Mother, as to the bow and who may handle it,
no man here has more authority than I.
Return to your room, Mother.

PENELOPE:

Telemachus—

TELEMACHUS [*speaking slowly*]:
Return to your own room, Mother,
and lock the door. Tend your spindle.
Tend your loom.

[PENELOPE *understands that* TELEMACHUS *is trying to tell her some-thing, and although she doesn't know what it is, she exits.* EUMAEUS *slyly closes the doors behind her.*]

        Eumaeus, give this man
Odysseus's bow. And here, for his bravery,
I give him my old cloak. They say it was
my father's, but now I know he's never
coming back.

[TELEMACHUS *takes off his cloak and puts it on* ODYSSEUS. *It fits him.* EUMAEUS *brings the bow.*]

SUITOR ONE [*to* EUMAEUS]:
        Ho! Where do you think
you're taking that, you smutty slave?

SUITOR TWO:
We'll toss you back among the pigs,
for your own dogs to eat!

[ODYSSEUS *takes the bow and weighs it in his hands.*]

SUITOR THREE:
Oh look, a lover of bows!

SUITOR FOUR:
Maybe he has one like it at home, in his own palace!

SUITOR FIVE:
Maybe he wants to make one himself!

SUITOR THREE:
May his fortune grow an inch for every inch he bends it!

[*Music: an ominous sound.*]

ATHENA:
But the man skilled in all ways of contending,
satisfied by the great bow's look and heft,
like a musician who with a quiet hand
draws between his thumb and forefinger
a sweet new string upon a peg: so effortlessly
Odysseus in one motion strung the bow.

[*He fires his arrow, with* ATHENA's *help, straight through the ax heads.*]

SUITORS [*variously*]:
Our arms!
        Where are the arms?
The door is bolted!
Our arms! Our arms!

ODYSSEUS:
        You yellow dogs!
You thought I'd never make it home from Troy!
You dared bid for my wife while I was still alive?

Contempt was all you had for the gods who rule wide heaven.
Contempt was all you had for what men would say of you.

ATHENA:
Odysseus stood at one end of the hall,
Athena at the other, and the slaughter began.

[*New music. One by one the* SUITORS *are slaughtered by* ODYSSEUS,
TELEMACHUS, ATHENA, *and even* EUMAEUS. *Three* MAIDS *are also
killed. All the dead are led away by* HERMES. *(For additional staging
suggestions, see the appendix, page 171.)*]

PENELOPE AND ODYSSEUS

[PENELOPE'*s bedroom.* EURYCLEIA *enters. Music ends.*]

EURYCLEIA:
                                                Wake!
Wake up, dear child! Penelope, come down,
see with your own eyes what all these years you longed for!
Odysseus is here! Oh, in the end, he came!
And he has killed your suitors, killed them all!

PENELOPE [*drowsy*]:
Dear Nurse, the gods have touched you.
You always had good sense; but now they've
touched you.

EURYCLEIA:

        It is true, true, as I tell you!
He has come! That stranger they were baiting
was Odysseus. Telemachus knew it days ago—

PENELOPE:

Dear Nurse, dear Nurse, listen to me—
if he came home in secret, as you say,
how could he engage them singlehanded? How?
They were all down there, every one.

EURYCLEIA:

I didn't see it; I only heard the groans
of dying men—until Telemachus came to my door.
Then I came out and found Odysseus
erect, with the dead men littering the floor
this way and that. Here is your prayer, your passion,
granted! Your own lord lives, he is at home,
he found you safe, he found his son—

PENELOPE:

                Do not lose yourself

in this rejoicing; wait: you know
how splendid that return would be—
but it isn't possible. If the suitors are dead
as you say, then some god has killed them,
a god, sick of their arrogance.
But the true person of Odysseus?
He lost his home, he died far from Ithaca.

EURYCLEIA:
Child, he's downstairs by the fire!
Come down! I stake my life on it, he's here!
Let me die in agony if I lie!

[*Music.* ATHENA *enters, and as she begins to speak,* PENELOPE *leaves her room and comes down to the hall.* ODYSSEUS *is sitting quietly at the far side of the room.*]

ATHENA:
Penelope turned to descend the stairs, her heart
in tumult. Had she better keep her distance
and question him, her husband? Should she run
up to him, take his hands, and kiss him now?
Crossing the door sill she sat down against
the wall, across the room from the lord Odysseus.
There sat the man and never lifted up his eyes.

ODYSSEUS:
Never pressed himself on her.

[TELEMACHUS *enters. Music ends.*]

TELEMACHUS:
                              Mother,
cruel Mother, do you feel nothing? How can you
keep yourself apart this way from Father?

PENELOPE:
                                        I am stunned, child,
I cannot speak to him. I cannot question him.
I cannot keep my eyes upon his face.

If really he is Odysseus, truly home,
beyond all doubt we two shall know each other
better than you or anyone. There are
secret signs we know, we two.

TELEMACHUS:
Mother, this is—

ODYSSEUS:
Leave us, Telemachus.

[TELEMACHUS *exits.* PENELOPE *sits at the far end of the hall from*
ODYSSEUS.]

               Strange woman,
the immortals of Olympus made you hard,
harder than any. Who else in the world
would keep aloof as you do from her husband
after twenty years?

PENELOPE:
               Strange man,
if man you are. . . . This is no pride on my part
nor scorn for you—not even wonder.
I know so well how you—how he—appeared
boarding the ship for Troy. But all the same . . .

[*She stands and makes as though to leave.*]

I'll have Eurycleia make up your bed,
But place it in the hall, outside the bedchamber—

ODYSSEUS:

Woman! By heaven have you betrayed me?
Who dared uproot my bed? I made that
bed from an olive tree that grew like a pillar
on the building plot. I built the room around it.
Inlaid it with gold and silver and shaped it
into a bedpost, then made three others like it.
My bed cannot be moved into a hall!
No one has ever seen that room—

PENELOPE:

Odysseus, Odysseus, Odysseus,
what sign could be so clear? You know our bed;
our secret bed. Odysseus, it's you. It's you.
Do not rage at me. I could not welcome you
with love on sight! I armed myself
long ago against the frauds of men,
imposters who might come. But you make
my stiff heart know that I am yours.

[*Music.* ODYSSEUS *and* PENELOPE *embrace.* ATHENA *slowly unties and
removes her golden sandals as she speaks.*]

ATHENA:

Now from his breast into his eyes the ache
of longing mounted, and he wept at last,
his dear wife, clear and faithful, in his arms,
longed for
                as the sun-warmed earth is longed for by a swimmer
spent in rough water where his ship went down
under Poseidon's blows, gale winds, and tons of sea.
Few men can keep alive through a big surf

to crawl, clotted with brine, on kindly beaches
in joy, in joy, knowing the abyss behind:
and so she too rejoiced, her gaze upon her husband,
her white arms round him pressed as though forever.

[*Music ends.*]

ZEUS [*whispering from above*]:
My daughter, the fresh dawn is stirring, she beckons
to come forward from her bed of paling ocean.

ATHENA [*whispering back*]:
Hold her back this once; let this night linger.
They are reveling in love and stories. She will
not rest until she has heard all his tale.

[*All exit.*]

LAERTES

[*The sound of birds.* LAERTES, ODYSSEUS's *aged father, enters with a little spade and a basket of seedlings. He sits and begins to plant.* ODYSSEUS *enters and regards him for a moment.*]

ODYSSEUS:
                               Old man, the orchard keeper
you work for is no townsman. He has a good eye
for growing things; there's not a nursling,
fig tree, olive tree, or garden bed uncared for
on this farm. But I might add—don't take offense—

your own appearance could be tidier. Old age,
yes—but why the squalor? But tell me,
whose land is this? Is it Ithaca? Some time
ago I entertained a visitor from abroad; he said
he was the son of Laertes. Do you know the man?

LAERTES:
You've come to that man's island, right enough,
but your trip has been in vain. Odysseus did
not come home from Troy, and his palace is filled
with fools and criminals. He was my son—
if I ever had a son.
                              Ah, far
from those who loved him, far from his native land;
in some sea the fish have picked his bones. His mother
at his bier never bewailed him, nor did I, his father,
nor did his admirable wife, Penelope, who should
have closed her husband's eyes. So much is due the dead.

ODYSSEUS [approaching]:
Old man, will you look at something?
Do you see this scar? I was wounded here
by the white tusk of a boar when I went hunting
on Parnassos. My mother and my father sent
me to visit my grandparents, and sent their swineherd
with me.
               I tricked you, sir, when I said I didn't
know this place. You brought me here yourself,
when I was a small boy at your heels, and you

taught me the names of all these trees.
You gave me thirteen pear, ten apple, and forty fig trees,
and you pointed to the fifty rows of vines
that were to come to me and said,
"Look here, Odysseus, my little son,
I've planted these so each row will bloom in turn,
and bunches of every hue will hang here ripening,
weighted down"—

LAERTES:
"weighted down"—

LAERTES AND ODYSSEUS:
"by the god of summer days."

ODYSSEUS:
Do you remember this, my father?

LAERTES:
Odysseus? But how? Odysseus—?

ODYSSEUS [*pulling him up, embracing him*]:
I will tell you everything, my honorable father.
But back to the palace now.
Resume your rightful place.

[ODYSSEUS *and* LAERTES *exit.*]

CONCLUSION

[*Drums in the distance.* ATHENA *enters and addresses* ZEUS.]

ATHENA:
O Father of us all and King of Kings,
enlighten me: the fathers and brothers of all
those slaughtered suitors are assembling, demanding
vengeance against Odysseus. What is your secret will?
War and battle, worse and more of it,
or can you not impose a pact on both?

ZEUS [*descending from heaven*]:
My child, what strange remarks you make.
Did you not plan this action by yourself—
see to it that Odysseus, on his homecoming,
should have their blood?
                              Conclude it as you will.
There is one proper way, if I may say so:
Odysseus's honor being satisfied,
let him be made king by a sworn pact forever,
and we, for our part, will blot out the memory
of sons and brothers slain. As in the old time
let men of Ithaca henceforth be friends;
prosperity enough and peace attend them.

ATHENA:
An excellent plan, my father.

[ZEUS *exits. Music.* MUSE *enters and undresses* ATHENA *down to the
original clothes she wore as the* WOMAN *at the beginning of the*

play, but now she is a CHILD. ODYSSEUS *enters and crosses, carrying an oar. Music ends.*]

CHILD:
What is that you are carrying, sir, a winnowing fan?

ODYSSEUS [*stopping*]:
It is an oar.

CHILD:
What is an oar?

ODYSSEUS:
For rowing on the sea.

CHILD:
What is the sea?

[ODYSSEUS *plants his oar where he stands. He looks back at the* CHILD.]

A NOTE ON THE CASTING

The original division of roles among twenty-one actors is below. Your cast may be larger by a great many or perhaps smaller by one (an elderly actor just for Laertes may not be feasible), both of which would influence distribution of roles. Further reduction in cast size might make the play difficult—you'll be shorthanded on boats and not have a very intimidating number of suitors, unless you use female suitors.

The designation "sailor" below may indicate a sailor on the boats of Odysseus, Telemachus, Phaecia, or all three. Sometimes Odysseus will have as many as twelve sailors with him (island of Helios) and sometimes only four (Aeolus), depending on how many actors may be spared. Likewise, there might be between two and eight suitors in a scene to indicate the presence of suitors. Although the script indicates "Sailor One," "Sailor Two," and so on in many scenes, this does not mean that the same actor must always play Sailor One or Sailor Two from scene to scene. The same holds true for the suitors. All animals are played by actors.

FIRST WOMAN: Athena

SECOND WOMAN: Muse, Calypso, Companion to Nausicaa, Phaecian (Seabelt), Sailor, Enchanted Animal, Siren (Nun), Scylla, Argos

THIRD WOMAN: Penelope, Companion to Nausicaa, Phaecian (Bordalee), Sailor, Enchanted Animal, Siren (Teacher)

FOURTH WOMAN: Eurycleia, Companion to Nausicaa, Lotus Eater, Sailor, Odysseus's Mother, Siren (Nurse), Scylla

FIFTH WOMAN: Denizen of Heaven, Maid (Alcippe), Sailor, Eidothea, Companion to Nausicaa, Phaecian (Seareach), Lotus Eater, Sheep, Circe, Scylla, Sheep on Helios

SIXTH WOMAN: Maid, Townsperson, Sailor, Nausicaa, Lotus Eater, Sheep, Siren (Girl Scout), Scylla

SEVENTH WOMAN: Maid (Melantho), Helen, Drummer, Companion to Nausicaa, Phaecian, Siren (Businesswoman)

EIGHTH WOMAN: Phemios, Arete, Lotus Eater, Sailor (Eurylochus), Siren (Bride)

FIRST MAN: Odysseus

SECOND MAN: Zeus, Cyclops (Polyphemus), Demodocus

THIRD MAN: Telemachus, Drummer, Lotus Eater, Enchanted Animal

FOURTH MAN: Antinous, Phaecian, Sailor

FIFTH MAN: Aeolus, Teiresias, Eumaeus

SIXTH MAN: Suitor, Sailor, Young Menelaus, Hermes, Phaecian (Sternman), First Neighboring Cyclops

SEVENTH MAN: Halitherses, Alcinous, Sailor

EIGHTH MAN: Suitor (Eurymachus), Mentor, Menelaus, Sailor, Phaecian (Bluewater)

NINTH MAN: Suitor, Proteus, Drummer, Phaecian (Hullman), Lotus Eater, Sheep

TENTH MAN: Suitor (Leodes), Sailor (Perimedes), Eteonus, Phaecian (Tideracer)

ELEVENTH MAN: Suitor, Sailor, Neoman, Phaecian (Laodamas), Elpenor

TWELFTH MAN: Poseidon, Suitor, Sailor, Phaecian (Beacher), Second Neighboring Cyclops

THIRTEENTH MAN: Laertes

APPENDIX: ORIGINAL STAGING OF CYCLOPS, THE UNDERWORLD, THE DEATH OF THE SUITORS, BOATS, AND FLYING

As both the adapter and director of this version of *The Odyssey*, I found it difficult to gauge how much stage direction to put in the body of the script. To avoid being overly prescriptive to a potential director, and for the sake of the reader who wants to fall into the events of the story without being burdened by how we achieved those events onstage, I have kept stage directions to a minimum. I've indicated only the major music cues (of the original three hundred plus) and almost no lighting cues (of more than five hundred plus). However, what follows is some technical description that might be useful or interesting to someone thinking of producing or directing the play.

The Cyclops in the original production was made to look huge by being played in shadow upstage of a big white curtain. The life-size sailors approached the curtain, were "grabbed" by the Cyclops from behind, and dragged under. Then the actor playing the Cyclops held up two small toy soldiers that he could rip apart and "devour" in enlarged silhouette. Similarly, the bowl of wine Odysseus offered was large when the audience saw it, but set behind the drop was an identical but very small version of that bowl. This second bowl appeared tiny in the silhouetted Cyclops's hands. After he was blinded, the Cyclops came out from behind the curtain, "brought down to size," and he staggered after a very small model boat manipulated by Athena while the life-size boat (consisting of actors in chairs in formation, rowing with bamboo poles) occupied another part of the stage.

For his trip to the Underworld, Odysseus stepped downstage, and the downstage set of walls closed behind him. When he said, "And this is how I, a living man, went into the Underworld," the walls slid away to reveal, projected across the entirety of the upstage cyclorama, an enormous close-up filmed image of a woman's face perpetually turning toward and away from the audience. This image of the mournful woman continued throughout the entirety of the scene. There was a microphone midstage, and the figure of a woman crouched upstage, her back to the audience. On a tattered piece of fabric hanging downstage right, the moving image of Elpenor was projected as Elpenor himself appeared onstage. His voice was amplified or mixed into the music. When he left, he pulled the tattered curtain off behind him so that the image fell into nothingness and disappeared. When Teiresias appeared, he wore a white robe with enormous sleeves. He delivered his speech at the microphone with filmed images of himself—his bandaged eyes, his hands—projected onto his body and outspread arms. When the woman crouching upstage turned and revealed herself as Odysseus's mother, we saw that she was the woman in the large, perpetual film. All the spirits' voices were amplified or recorded. At the end of the scene all sound and filmed images snapped off as bright lights filled the stage.

The death of the suitors in the great hall was staged as follows: the suitors were led, one by one, into an individual pool of light. Far above each of their heads a small canvas bag filled with sand was lowered into view. The suitors sadly removed their armor and handed it off to either Telemachus or Eumaeus. Athena, with the help of Odysseus, reached up with her long spear and stabbed each bag, causing a thin stream of sand to pour down on each suitor, who slowly collapsed on the floor. At one point, sheets of sand rained down on the scene, particularly on the maids who were pulled onstage by Odysseus. The streams of sand were evocative of many things: "dust to dust," sand through an hourglass, the dirt thrown into a grave, and, through a trick of the eye, the spirits of the suitors ascending from their bodies. After all the suitors were dead, they stood up and stepped upstage. The sandbags dropped, and each suitor picked up his own bag and followed Hermes off. All of this was accompanied by strange, dark music: minor chords, thumps, the sound of breaking glass, and whispered voices recalling fragmentary moments of life.

Boats came and went with lightning speed: each sailor brought in a chair and a bamboo pole (his "oar"). He set the chair as part of a formation—a straight or diagonal line, a triangle, two lines, parallel or perpendicular to the proscenium, and so on. The sailors sat sometimes forward, sometimes backward, on their chairs; they reversed the direction of their chairs to indicate a reversal of direction of the boat. Rowing was done in a variety of ways: each sailor holding his bamboo pole in front of him and reaching out, then pulling it toward himself repeatedly or paddling as though in a kayak; or all sailors rowing on the right, or the left, or alternate sides. The boat was boarded by the sailors walking across the seats of the lined-up chairs or just by sitting down. These variations came into play because they suggested different types of boats, lands, or circumstances, or simply because they were expedient or pretty.

Flying of immortals, arrows, and spears was accomplished manually. Often, one actor carried Athena, his outstretched arms supporting her under her hips above his head; or she sat sideways across one of his shoulders, her arms free. Athena aided the flight of arrows and spears; she took them as they left the hand of Odysseus and carried them aloft to their destination. Sometimes things happened in slow motion to make things easier, as when Antinous throws the stool and Athena deflects it in midair.

Athena (Mariann Mayberry) presents Odysseus's case to Zeus (Ed Dixon) on Mount Olympus.

The suitors gather in the great hall.

Athena (Mariann Mayberry) tells Telemachus (Doug Hara), "You cannot go on clinging to your childhood."

Athena (Mariann Mayberry) flies away.

Helen (Anjali Bhimani) and Menelaus (Yasen Peyankov)

Odysseus (Christopher Donahue) weeps in the hall of the Phaecians.

The Cyclops (Ed Dixon) captures two sailors.

Odysseus (Christopher Donahue) pleads with Circe (Louise Lamson).

Odysseus (Christopher Donahue) sees his mother (Lisa Tejero) in the Underworld.

The Sirens (Felicity Jones, Anna Fitzwater, Anjali Bhimani, Julanne Chidi Hill, Christina Apathy, and Louise Lamson)

A sailor (Yasen Peyankov) eyes the sacred sheep (Louise Lamson) on the island of Helios.

Odysseus (Christopher Donahue) finds the slaughtered oxen.

Poseidon (Jonathan Partington)

Athena (Mariann Mayberry) greets Odysseus (Christopher Donahue) on Ithaca.

Odysseus (Christopher Donahue) cowers by Athena (Mariann Mayberry) as Antinous (Kyle Hall) throws a chair. Eumaeus (Gary Wingert) flees in the background.

Penelope (Felicity Jones) challenges the suitors to try Odysseus's bow.

Mariann Mayberry and the playwright

ABOUT THE PLAYWRIGHT

Mary Zimmerman's credits as an adapter and a director include *Metamorphoses, The Arabian Nights, Journey to the West, Eleven Rooms of Proust, The Notebooks of Leonardo da Vinci, The Secret in the Wings* (based on fairy tales), and *Mirror of the Invisible World* (from the Persian *Haft Paykar*). Her work has been produced at the Lookingglass Theatre and Goodman Theatre of Chicago; on Broadway at Circle in the Square; in New York at Second Stage, the Brooklyn Academy of Music, and the Manhattan Theatre Club; at the Mark Taper Forum in Los Angeles; and at the McCarter, Berkeley Repertory, and Seattle Repertory theaters as well as many others around the country and abroad. The recipient of a Tony Award for her direction of *Metamorphoses* and a MacArthur Fellowship, Zimmerman is a professor of performance studies at Northwestern University.